*beyond*ATTACHMENTS

makingmemories

attach : join, connect, fasten, put together,

add, tie, stick, adhere, bond

When it comes right down to it, attaching one thing to another pretty much sums up what crafters do. But it can be so much more than just gluing, taping and sticking. The perfect attachment can become the element that pulls your project together — literally.

In this book, you'll discover how to use familiar, everyday objects like staples, jump rings and bead chain, and old favorites like eyelets, brads and ribbon in unusual and unexpected ways. Plus, we're thrilled to introduce you to some of the latest, hottest products from the Making Memories™ family. You'll be delighted, surprised and ultimately, inspired to see what happens when you blend your imagination, your project supplies and innovative attachment ideas.

So get ready to fasten, tie, hammer, punch, fold, sew and twist your way to inspiring techniques and ideas. Get ready to go beyond attachments.

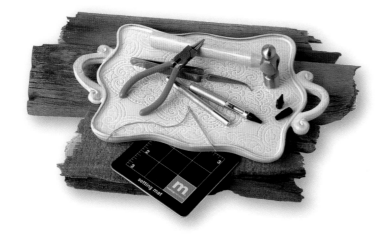

An old belief states that there's strength in numbers. That's definitely the case when it comes to attachments. While one single brad or length of ribbon might be all a design requires, there's a richness and intricacy when you combine, stack and layer two, three or even four pieces together. Use one or all of the following combinations to create the perfect additions to your projects.

1. Attach Bead Chain to project by adhering with Glue Dots or stringing through preset eyelets. Connect two Jump Rings and hang from chain. Tie a ribbon on one and dangle an Eyelet Alphabet letter and metal tag from the other. Brush the tag with acrylic paint and wipe off the excess leaving paint in letter grooves.

2. Cut a small tag shape from cardstock and punch a hole at the top. Paint the letters in a Washer Word and wipe off the excess. Set two sizes and types of eyelets in the washer and position stack over the tag, lining up the holes. Tie a string through and adhere to the page. Rub on a Simply Stated word.

3. Position a Shaped Clip and secure in place by using a small brad in the corner. Cut a section from a sheet of Defined, add stamps or memorabilia and tuck behind the clip.

4. Wrap a piece of ribbon around a key or other object. Set an eyelet near the end of the ribbon loop. Use a triangle Jump Ring to hang small tags from the end.

5. Set a Label Holder with snaps. Fill in the center with Diamond Glaze and carefully position individually cut letters on top. Wait for it to dry. Cut a strip of Ribbon Words and use staples to attach to the paper.

6. Crisscross coordinating lengths of ribbon through a Washer Word. Paint the letters in the washer and wipe off the excess. Slip memorabilia into place behind washer.

7. Wrap a stamp around the edge of the paper. Set three rows of eyelets. Thread wire through one side of the eyelets, string beads onto wire and loop through the eyelets on the other side.

8. Position Photo Anchors and set buttons on top. Sew the buttons through the holes in the Photo Anchors to hold them in place. Tie thread behind the paper.

9. Tear a piece of patterned paper and adhere to cardstock. Wrap ribbon through one side of a Ribbon Charm. Pull the end of the ribbon back on itself and secure in place with a snap. Repeat on the other side. For second buckle, weave one end of ribbon through, pull back on itself and glue together. Weave the other end of the ribbon through and tighten to close. Add a strip of lace.

10. Laminate a dried flower. Cut a piece of scrim fabric and fray edges. Use a Stick Pin to attach the flower and fabric to cardstock. Dangle a triangle Jump Ring through the end of the pin. Tie a ribbon at the end of the triangle.

11. Make a small envelope out of cardstock. On the flap, place a small button underneath a large button and stitch together in place. Repeat stacked buttons directly below on the envelope. Use twine or ribbon to wrap around buttons creating your own closure.

12. Secure a safety pin to page. Attach a Jump Ring at the end of the safety pin. Thread string through three tags and knot together on the Jump Ring. Let tags dangle loosely.

1

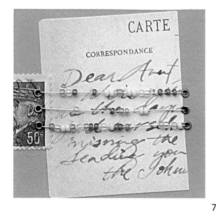

2

3

4

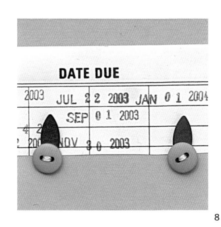

5

6

7

8

9

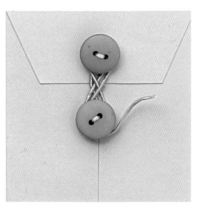

10

11

12

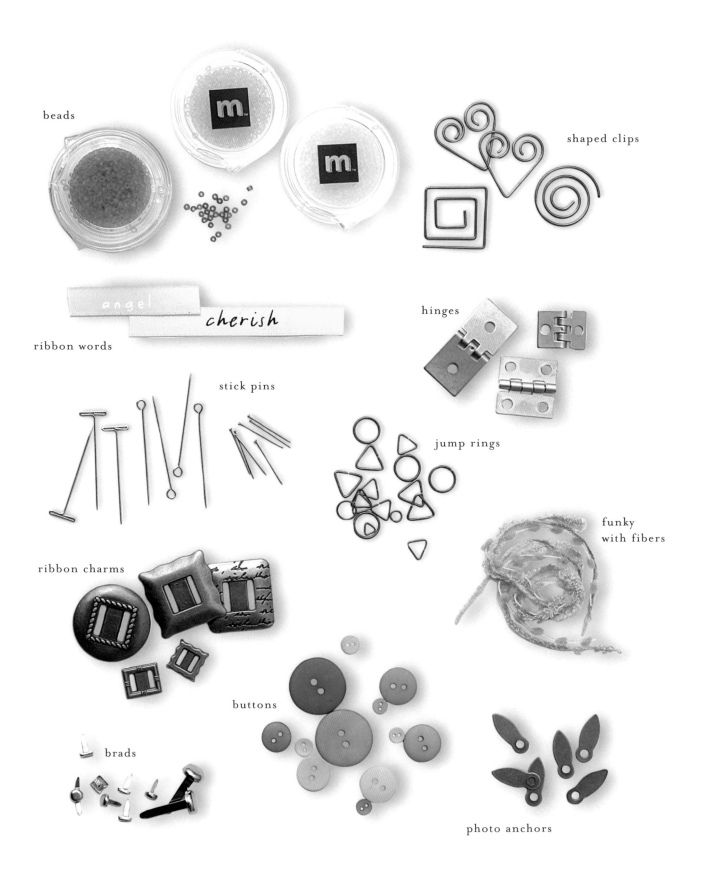

beads

shaped clips

ribbon words

hinges

stick pins

jump rings

funky
with fibers

ribbon charms

buttons

brads

photo anchors

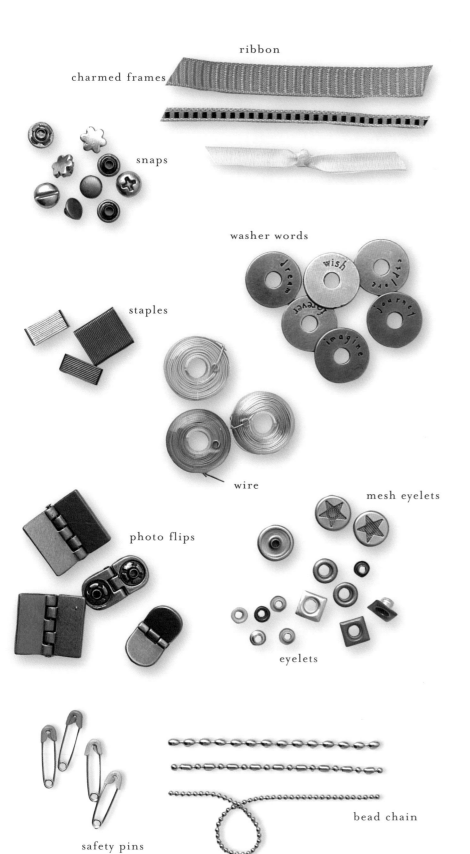

ribbon

charmed frames

snaps

washer words

staples

wire

photo flips

mesh eyelets

eyelets

safety pins

bead chain

CONTENTS

1

2

3a

3b

1 attaching photos

Just like a picture is worth a thousand words, there are at least a thousand different ways to attach one to a layout. Although we didn't have enough space for a thousand, in the following pages, our artists succeeded in sharing a wealth of ideas. You'll see angelic baby photos hung with sweet, miniature safety pins and rough, tough teenage boys draped in killer bead chain. Ribbons, washers, wire and more—you'll be amazed at what you can do.

If you've got photos to put on anything (and we're betting you do), this chapter is for you. Try out some of these ideas and mix in a few of your own—in the end, your projects will speak for themselves.

---

1 BIRTHDAY GIRL
By Heidi Swapp

Alphabet charm, eyelet phrase
and eyelets: Making Memories
Paper: Making Memories
Other: Ribbon and string

how to: *Frame three photos in three openings of Perspectives paper. Cut out. Mount on the page with eyelets and folded strips of cardstock. Make tabs on the titles, journaling block and photo with folded strips of cardstock set with eyelets. Set two eyelets on each side of the page. Thread string through the tabs, then tie the string across the page.*

2 PARTY INVITATION
By Heidi Swapp

Magnetic date stamp, photo flips
and washer word: Making Memories
Paint: Folk Art
Paper: Making Memories
Photo corners: Kolo
Ribbon: May Arts
Other: Alphabet stamps

how to: *Mount a photo on cardstock. Affix Photo Flips to the photo. Create the background for the invitation with cardstock circles and party information. Attach the photo to the background by setting the Photo Flips, making sure the photo covers the party information. Embellish with alphabet stamps and a Washer Word attached with ribbon.*

3a SIMPLY EMMA (cover)
By Heidi Swapp

Adhesive: Perfect Paper Adhesive,
USArtQuest
Brads and washer words: Making Memories
Paper: Making Memories
Other: Book paper and Plexiglas

how to: *Fold a piece of 12" x 6" in half, then cover with paper. Paint and ink as desired. Decoupage the surface with matte-finish Perfect Paper. Cut a piece of Plexiglas with utility scissors (the cuts and edges will not be perfect). Punch a hole in the top and bottom of the Plexiglas with an anywhere hole punch. Poke corresponding holes in the front cover of the book. Attach the Plexiglas over the photo using Washer Words and brads.*

3b SIMPLY EMMA (inside)
By Heidi Swapp

Alphabet stamps: PSX Design
Defined sticker, jump rings, page pebble
and shaped clips: Making Memories
Letter sticker: Anna Griffin
Stamping ink: Clearsnap
Other: Brads, lace trim, photo corner, sheet
music, silk flower and upholstery thread

how to: *Cut two pieces of 12" x 12" paper in half, then fold in half. Use upholstery thread and a large backstitch to stitch the pages together. Create photo holders with heart Shaped Clips fastened to the page with brads. On the right-hand page, wire a heart Shaped Clip to music paper, then adhere to the page. Attach the photo to the Shaped Clip with two jump rings. To create the music paper photo corner, stick a large, square Page Pebble to music paper, then cut in half at an angle. Adhere to the photo with an adhesive dot.*

1 REMINISCING
By Erin Terrell

Alphabet charms, charmed photo corners, eyelets, jump rings, metal frame, simply stated rub-ons and wire: Making Memories
Blue beads: Crafts Etc!
Green beads: CCA Jewelry Accents
Large heart charm: Leisure Arts Memories in the Making
Paint: Americana
Paper: Making Memories
Pen: EK Success
Photo-tinting oils: Marshall's Oils
Small heart charm: JewelCraft
Stamping ink: Clearsnap and Memories
Trim: me and my BIG ideas

how to: Hand tint photos, then mat on cardstock. Create a background using coordinating patterned papers and scraps from a brown tag. Age some of the papers with brown or green inks. Paint a Metal Frame with acrylic paint, then frame a section of the patterned paper. Set eyelets next to some of the photos. String beads on wire and wrap the wire around the tip of an embossing stylus to create the kinks. Poke each end of the wire through the eyelets, then secure on the back with tape, covering the sharp ends. Hang heart charms from the wire using jump rings. Create the title with Alphabet Charms. Add white acrylic paint to the Alphabet Charms and heart charms.

2 TINY SOUL
By Kris Stanger

Adhesive: Glue Pen, Making Memories
Buttons, eyelet charms, eyelet letters, page pebble, safety pins and scrapbook stitches: Making Memories
Paint: Delta
Paper: Making Memories
Silk ribbon: Bucilla
Other: Chenille

how to: Sketch a pattern for the ribbon background. Glue down the silk ribbon with a Glue Pen (it won't go through the ribbon like many other adhesives). Tape the ends of the ribbon to the back of the layout. Stitch buttons to page where ribbons cross. Arrange the photos, making sure not to cover too much of the photo with the ribbon. Fold a scrap of chenille around one side of the layout and embellish with safety pins and star Eyelet Charms.

Kris' tip: Have a baby blue vignette put around black and white photos for a fun "baby boy" effect!

3

3 YOU MAKE ME A BETTER PERSON
By Stephanie McAtee

Alphabet stamps: PSX Design
Aluminum posts: Paper Source
Bead chain, metal sheet and staples:
Making Memories
Paint: Americana
Watch face: 7gypsies
Other: Bottle caps, button, cardboard,
fabric, galvanized steel, library card,
library pocket, number stencils, paper
clip and soda-can tab

how to: *For the right-hand page, paint
cardboard with acrylic paint, then attach
fabric to the top with adhesive dots.
Journal on a library card and slip it
in a library pocket. Use cardboard for
the left-hand page to accommodate
the thickness of the posts. Punch holes
for the posts, then stick the posts in
the holes. String Bead Chain around
the posts, going from one side to the
next. Wrap the edges of the photos
with pieces from a Metal Sheet.
Attach photos to the chain with
smaller pieces of Bead Chain.*

4

4 VACATION ON THE VERANDA
By Rhonda Solomon

Adhesive: Diamond Glaze, JudiKins
Beads, eyelet alphabet, eyelet charms,
metal word, ribbon charm, safety pins,
snaps, staples and washer words:
Making Memories
Paint: Delta
Photo corners: Boston International Inc.
Rubber stamps: Hero Arts, Hot Potato,
Inkadinkado, JudiKins and Rubber Monger
Stamping ink: Marvy
Other: Fabric and ribbon

how to: *Tape off four squares on the
left-hand page. Dry brush with acrylic
paints. Allow to dry, then carefully
remove the tape. Paint the flower and
circle Eyelet Charms. Rub paint on
Washer Words. Rubber stamp the title
on the circle Eyelet Charm, background
and fabric. Zigzag stitch fabric to the
background. Mat the main photo, then
attach with snaps and Washer Words.
Rubber stamp a slide mount on green
paper, cut out the inside and add Eyelet
Alphabet letters. Add photos to the
right side of layout. Print journaling on
painted paper and fabric.*

1 BEAUTY
By Robin Johnson

Eyelets, ribbon charm and paper tag:
Making Memories
Metal corner pieces: Boutique Trims
Paper: Perspectives, Making Memories;
7gypsies
Walnut ink: Anima Designs
Other: Decorative trim and ribbon

how to: *Tear around the outside edges of a one-opening Perspectives sheet. Chalk all sides to age. Set eyelets at the top and bottom of the opening. Run decorative trim through the eyelets, adding a small tag to the right side. Adhere the ends of the trim to the back of the paper. Adhere Perspectives paper to blue cardstock. Position photo in place. Cut a slit above and below the photo and run a ribbon around the photo and behind the blue paper. Tie off ribbon with a Ribbon Charm. Hand write the title with a flat brush and walnut ink. Add paper corner accents. Paint metal corner embellishments and adhere in place.*

2 LIFE'S LITTLE MOMENTS
By Robin Johnson

Alphabet stamps: PSX Design
Paper: Making Memories
Ribbon charm, paper tag and washer word:
Making Memories
Ribbon: Making Memories and Offray
Stamping ink: Ranger Industries
Tag: Avery

how to: *Make a box from chipboard. Cover the sides and bottom with patterned paper. Cut an additional piece of chipboard to the size of the lid. Tear a piece of patterned paper and glue in place. Cut off a pocket from an old pair of Levi's. Adhere pocket in place and stitch around the side and bottom seams to secure. Stitch around the outer edge of the chipboard. Glue embellished chipboard to the cover of the box. Wipe a Washer Word with paint, making sure it gets in the grooves. Wipe off any excess paint. Embellish the cover as desired.*

3 LITTLE THINGS CARD
By Robin Johnson

Buttons, stick pins and paper tag:
Making Memories
Paper: Making Memories
Ribbon: Offray
Other: Canvas paper

Fold a piece of 8 1/2" x 11" paper in half. Add a quotation to the card. Glue a strip of torn paper to the folded edge. Tie twine around the cover and tie it through two buttons. Cut a photo to a 1 1/2" square. Adhere the photo to a piece of canvas. Cut around the photo, leaving a small border. Put Stick Pins across the corners of the photo. Add a triangle jump ring to the end of one of the pins. Tie ribbon, tag and twine to the jump ring.

4 BABY ANNOUNCEMENT
By Robin Johnson

Label holder, safety pins: Making Memories
Paper: Making Memories
Photography: Dave Tevis
Ribbon: Offray

how to: *Divide an 8 1/2" x 11" piece of paper in half. Design the card on the computer so the baby's information prints on the inside panel. Print two cards at a time on the 8 1/2" x 11" sheet. Cut paper in half, then fold each card in half. Cut a hole in the front panel that is 3" x 3 1/2". Using a micro punch, make small holes in the top of the photo and in the top edge of the card. Attach the photo to the card with safety pins. Insert a word behind a label holder. Tie label holder with ribbon and adhere to card. Die cut an envelope from printed paper.*

5 FOR SUCH A SHORT TIME
By Jennifer Jensen

Adhesive: Mod Podge, Plaid
Computer font: Bookman Antiqua
Eyelet charm, eyelet letters, magnetic date stamp, metal sheet, metal words and photo anchors: Making Memories
Paint: Delta
Paper: Making Memories
Other: Buttons, doily, lace, photo mat, silk flower, tissue paper and tulle

how to: *Use Photo Anchors to secure the photo to the layout. Add a button to each anchor for added interest.*

5

1 **CHLOE**
By Jennifer Jensen

Adhesive: Mod Podge, Plaid
Alphabet stamps: PSX Design
Defined sticker, eyelet charms, eyelets,
magnetic date stamp, metal-rimmed
tags, stick pin and wire: Making Memories
Paint: Delta
Paper: Anna Griffin
Other: Beads, lace, letter tiles, ribbon,
sequins and tissue paper

how to: *Randomly sew ribbon and
lace to cardstock. Decoupage Defined
stickers underneath the center strip of
pink ribbon. Decoupage pink tissue
paper onto thin, white cardboard, then
glue painted tag Eyelet Charms to the
side. Glue a photo over the top. Attach
cardboard embellishment to the layout
by wiring beads to the Eyelet Charms,
then running the wire through an eyelet
in the background paper. Raise one of the
photos with pop-dots so the journaling
can slide underneath.*

2 **SISTERS, FRIENDS
AND PLAYMATES**
By Emily Waters

Defined sticker, eyelet shapes, hinges,
label holders, ribbon, safety pins, simply
stated rub-ons and washer words:
Making Memories
Paper: Making Memories
Other: Fabric and silk flower

how to: *Cut up and apply a Simply
Stated rub-on, letter by letter, to create
desired title. Sew a piece of fabric to the
corner. Sand and paint a golf ball Eyelet
Shape, then attach it to the center of a
silk flower. Glue to fabric corner. Cut a
photo in half and attach the two outer
sides to the layout with hinges so the
photos open from the inside out. Create
a word collage underneath the photos.
Attach remaining photos where desired,
adding little accents of ribbon, Washer
Words and label holders.*

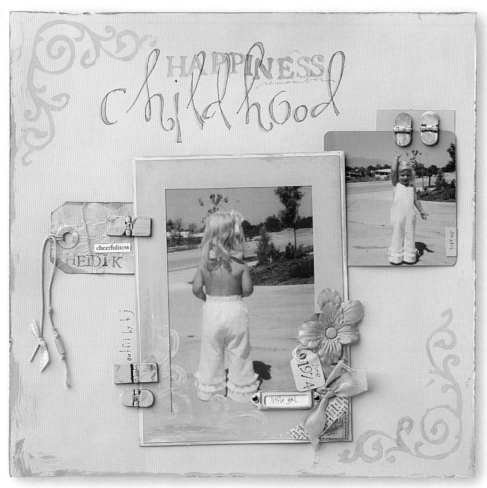

3 CHILDHOOD HAPPINESS
By Heidi Swapp

Alphabet stamps: PSX Design
Charmed photo corner, defined sticker,
label holder, photo flips, snap and staples:
Making Memories
Paint: Folk Art
Paper: Making Memories
Tags: American Tag
Others: Book paper, foam stamp,
silk flowers and silk ribbon

how to: *Create a frame using a 4"x 6"*
opening from Perspectives paper.
Embellish with ribbon, flowers and a
Charmed Photo Corner. Mount Photo
Flips to the photo frame, then set on
the background paper. Dab acrylic paint
on the Photo Flips. Use paint as the
stamping ink for the foam and alphabet
stamps.

4 EASTER MEMORIES
By Lynne Montgomery

Paint: DecoArt
Photo tape: 3L
Simply stated rub-ons and staples:
Making Memories
Varnish: Right Step Varnish, J.W. etc.
Wooden frame: Provo Craft
Other: Jelly beans and metal tins

how to: *Adhere photos to a wooden*
frame with photo tape. Lightly dry
brush over the photos with acrylic
paint. Apply Simply Stated rub-ons
and staple the photo edges with Color
Staples. Apply a thin coat of varnish
over the entire frame. Fill metal tins
with accents and slide into the center
of the frame.

Lynne's tip: Since the staples have a
difficult time going through several
layers and into the wood, avoid placing
the adhesive right on the photo's edge
when you initially adhere the photos
to the frame. In addition, add staples
before varnishing.

2 attaching titles

Titles are perhaps the hardest working elements on a scrapbook page. We depend on them to create a mood, illicit a reaction, evoke a memory, provide information and sum up the layout in just a few words. But they don't have to do all the heavy lifting alone.

Our artists will show you how using eye-catching embellishments to attach your titles can actually help reinforce the theme of your layout. A well-placed washer with just the right expression or a beaded wire strung through dangling letters are just the kind of touches that give more meaning, depth and substance to pages. As subtle as a paper clip or as practical as a hinge, thoughtful attachments can be a welcome companion to your titles and give them a much-needed break.

1 FAMILY BUILDING BLOCKS
By Julie Turner

Adhesive: Modeling glue, Citadel Modeling; Perfect Paper Adhesive, USArtQuest; PVA, Books By Hand
Computer font: Arial Narrow
Elastic: Darice
Eyelet charms, safety pins and shaped clips: Making Memories
Leather paper: K & Company
Linen hinging tape: Lineco
Metal stamps: Pittsburgh
Other: Book board, transparencies and wooden blocks

how to: *Fashion a box using six squares of book board. Fit the pieces together with linen hinging tape so the sides fall open. Cover the inside and outside of the box with leather paper. Hold the box closed with elastic ties and Shaped Clips. (Note: Be sure to make the box slightly larger so the blocks will still fit inside after you add the decorative paper.) To make the blocks, choose up to six photos for each block. Reduce the photos to size. For variety, use colored paper or a quotation on one of the sides instead of a photo. Attach the photos and papers with Perfect Paper.*

Julie's note: These blocks can be an alternative form of a photo album that can make an interesting conversation piece sitting on a coffee table or shelf. The blocks give an overview of one's family life without having to look through volumes of albums!

2 JOURNEY
By Julie Turner

Computer font: Arial Narrow
Elastic: Darice
Eyelet charms, eyelets, hinges, safety pin, shaped clip, simply stated rub-on and snaps: Making Memories
Leather paper: K & Company
Metal stamps: Pittsburgh
Other: Archival plastic cut from a Generations page keeper

how to: *Stamp words on leather paper with metal letter stamps. Apply a Simply Stated rub-on to plastic. Attach to the page with hinges. Place the journaling under the plastic.*

3 BEAUTY BOOK
By Julie Turner

Brads, simply stated rub-ons and washer words: Making Memories
Elastic: Darice
Linen hinging tape: Lineco
Other: Archival plastic cut from a Generations page keeper

how to: *Using linen hinging tape, piece together photos to make the inside book cover. Cut an outer cover from plastic. Score two folds in the middle about 3/4" apart to make a spine. Add a title using a Simply Stated rub-on. To make the inside pages, cut cardstock just smaller than the plastic cover. Score and fold a spine to match the cover. Create the binding by punching holes through all the layers. Insert brads and Washer Words to hold the book together. Snip the ends of the brads. The closure is made from black elastic cord and a Washer Word.*

4 SIX DAYS MINI BOOK
By Julie Turner

Computer font: Arial Narrow
Eyelet charms and safety pins: Making Memories
Leather paper: K & Company
Linen hinging tape: Lineco
Tag: American Tag
Other: Letters cut from a magazine and transparency

how to: *Punch two additional holes in two square Eyelet Charms to make the book covers. If the metal bends while punching the holes, gently tap it flat again. Create an accordion-folded pleat from leather paper. Trim to fit the square. Punch holes in each layer of the leather paper to match the holes in the metal covers. Attach the covers to the accordion-folded binding with tape. Place safety pins through all the holes to bind the book. To create the inside pages, cut photos to size. Attach two photos together using linen hinging tape. The tape will form the outside edge of the page. Attach the inside edge of the page to the binding folds with tape. Print journaling onto a transparency and insert it into the binding. Tie a mini tag to one of the safety pins.*

1 DIXIE CHICKS
By Rhonda Solomon

Eyelet quotes, eyelets, label holders, ribbon charms, safety pin and washer words: Making Memories
Paper: Making Memories
Rubber stamps: A Lost Art, Anna Griffin, Hero Arts, PSX Design and Rubber Monger
Stamping ink: Marvy
Other: Buttons, corrugated paper, photo corners and ribbon

how to: *Rubber stamp each letter of the title on a separate background. Adhere the letters on corrugated paper. Attach the title block to cardstock with ribbon. Mat photos and place on left side of layout along with other journaling and accents. Idea to note: Because the ticket was not the right color, Rhonda photocopied it onto a coordinating sheet of cardstock.*

2 BECKONING WAVES
By Robin Johnson

Eyelet and washer word: Making Memories
Paint: Delta
Stamping ink: Tsukineko
Tag: Avery
Tape: 3M

how to: *Trim tan paper to fit inside the burgundy paper. Chalk or ink the edges of the tan paper to age. Tear triangles of two different colors, then place behind the photo. Tear tape to hold the photo corners down. Ink the edges of the tape. Dip the tag in walnut ink, crinkle, then let dry. Hand letter a title on the tag. Wipe a Washer Word with paint, making sure the paint fills in the letter grooves. Wipe off excess paint. Place the tag behind the Washer Word, then secure the washer in place with an eyelet. Paint the rim of the eyelet.*

3 WELCOME BABY CARD
By Erin Terrell

Buttons, charmed plaque, scrapbook
stitches and simply stated mini:
Making Memories
Letters: FoofaLa
Paint: Americana
Paper: Making Memories and Daisy D's
Silk ribbon: Offray
Stamping ink: Clearsnap
Other: Silk flower

how to: *Cut a 12" x 12" piece of brown
cardstock to 6" x 12". Score and fold
one side of the cardstock 3" in and one
side 4" in. Decorate the 3" portion with
brown patterned paper. Decorate the
4" portion with pink patterned paper,
wrapping it around to the back of the
card. Paint the edges of the Charmed
Plaque with white acrylic paint, then
mat on pink cardstock. Ink the edges
of the alphabet letters with brown ink,
then stitch the alphabet to the card with
Scrapbook Stitches and buttons. Rub on
the Simply Stated words at the bottom
of the card. Wrap ribbon around the
card to hold it shut and adhere a silk
flower next to the ribbon.*

4 THE LAUGHTER OF GIRLS
By Heidi Swapp

Beads: Making Memories and
Designs by Pamela
Charmed photo corners, eyelet shape,
jump rings, metal-rimmed tag, scrapbook
stitches and staples: Making Memories
Paper: Making Memories and Anna Griffin
Vellum: Making Memories
Other: Book tape, fabric and silk ribbon

how to: *Print title onto book tape. Cut
into pieces, then attach together with
jump rings. Randomly place beads on
the jump rings. Hook the title to the
photos and the edges of the layout
with jump rings.*

1 TIDBITS
By Jennifer Jensen

Alphabet stamps: PSX Design
Metal sheets and shaped clips:
Making Memories
Paint: Delta
Paper: Making Memories
Silk ribbon: Bucilla
Other: Button and Velcro

how to: Fold patterned paper to form
an envelope. Rub the surface with
sandpaper until slightly worn. Glue a
button to the top flap and add a Velcro
dot underneath the top flap. Rub
acrylic paint over a strip cut from a
Metal Sheet. Rubber stamp a word on
the metal and punch a hole in each
end. Attach the title with ribbon and
Shaped Clips.

2a ASPIRE TO BE (cover)
By Jennifer Jensen

Adhesive: Mod Podge, Plaid
Alphabet stamps: PSX Design
Eyelet charm, eyelet letters, jump rings,
label holder, page pebbles, ribbon charms
and scrapbook stitches: Making Memories
Paint: Delta
Silk ribbon: Bucilla
Other: Beads, buttons and trim

how to: To make the cover frame, cut
a square in the cover of a book with an
X-Acto knife. Cut another square—just
smaller than the first—through about 10
pages, just under the cover. Repeat the
second step once more to complete the
frame. Glue and decoupage the pages
together, then glue a photo underneath.
Decorate the rest of the cover and the
spine as desired. For the inside pages,
sew approximately 10-20 pages together,
making one "page" to work on. Alter the
pages by adding embellishments, photos
and journaling.

2b BE TRUE (inside)
By Jennifer Jensen

Alphabet charms, defined stickers, eyelet
letters and page pebbles: Making Memories
Paint: Delta
Rick rack: Wright's
Silk ribbon: Bucilla
Other: Book paper, button and ribbon

how to: Sew ribbon and rick rack directly
onto the book pages. Rub acrylic paint
over the Alphabet Charms and Eyelet
Letters. Rub excess paint off the
Alphabet Charms. Add Page Pebbles
to the tops of the charms. Glue the
letters to the page.

3 SEVEN YEARS OF SMILES
By Jennifer Jensen

Adhesive: Mod Podge, Plaid
Alphabet stamps: PSX Design
Computer font: Type Upright
Eyelet charms, jump rings, metal
sheet, page pebbles, safety pins
and snaps: Making Memories
Paper: Making Memories and
Paper Adventures
Other: Altoid tin and rhinestone

how to: Paint the inside and outside
of a round Altoid tin. Trim a photo and
velveteen paper to fit inside. Cut flower
designs from a Metal Sheet. Paint the
flowers and add to the top of the tin.
Make a chain from safety pins and
jump rings to attach the title.

4 SEVEN YEAR SIGNIFICANCE
By Jennifer Jensen

Adhesive: Mod Podge, Plaid
Alphabet stamps: PSX Design
Brads, eyelet charm, eyelet letters,
jump rings, label holder, metal mesh,
snaps, staples, stick pins and wire
mesh: Making Memories
Paint: Delta
Paper: Making Memories
Other: Book covers, fabric, flowers, piece
from an old blotter desk set, tape measure,
upholstery tacks and wooden box

how to: Remove the hinges from a
wooden box and use only the bottom
part. Construct a lid from the cover of
a large book, gluing the spine of the
book cover to the side of the box. Cover
the spine and part of the lid with fabric.
Secure with small nails. Staple Metal
Mesh to the top of the book cover and
wrap it underneath to the back. Cut a
square in another book cover to use as
a frame on the top of the box. Decoupage
words from an old book around the
frame. Cover the rest of the box with
patterned paper and cover the inside
with fabric.

5 LOLA CORBRIDGE
By Emily Waters

Alphabet charms, brads, jump rings,
magnetic alphabet stamp, ribbon,
ribbon charms, safety pins, simply
stated rub-ons, staples and washer
words: Making Memories
Alphabet stamps: Making Memories
Perspectives: Making Memories
Other: Envelope, mini tag and old
book paper

how to: Place old book paper behind
the three Perspective openings. Mount
photos on cardstock, then place on book
paper. Wrap book paper around the right
side of the large photo opening and staple
in place. Attach silk flower with a brad.
Wrap ribbon around the layout and tie
in a knot. Attach a mini tag with a book
ring and safety pin to the ribbon. Attach
to an envelope. To create the title, tear
and fold down a portion of cardstock.
Using Simply Stated rub-ons, cut out
individual letters to make the title. Wrap
ribbon around the fold and attach with
a brad and Washer Word. Staple accents
of book paper to the corners. Adhere
small Alphabet Charms to the inside
of small Ribbon Charms to create a
framed look.

1 LAKE POWELL SUMMER FUN
By Heidi Swapp

Charmed photo corners, eyelet alphabet, eyelet phrases, eyelets, hinges and photo flips: Making Memories
Tag: Avery

how to: *Arrange the photos on the layout. Choose three photos to cover with title blocks and to hinge to the page. Punch a small square from each block to reveal the photo underneath. Embellish with tags, Eyelet Words, Eyelet Phrases and Eyelet Alphabets.*

2 CHICAGO SUBWAY
By Stephanie McAtee

Adhesive: Diamond Glaze, JudiKins
Jewelry findings: Karmul Studios
Magnetic date stamp, metal-rimmed tag, metal sheet and staples: Making Memories
Paint: Americana
Paper: Making Memories
Silver rings and rivets: Rusty Pickle
Transfer paper: Lazertran
Vintage photo: ARTchix Studio
Walnut ink: Anima Designs
Waxed linen: 7gypsies
Other: Cardboard, fabric, glassine envelope, paper pieces and old book fabric

how to: *Remove the vellum from the inside of a metal-rimmed tag and use it to frame the train. Cover the train with a light coat of Diamond Glaze to make it stand out. Frame the photo of the three ladies with a Metal Sheet, then cover with Diamond Glaze. Make a matchbook-style mini book from cardboard, then sew photo sleeves to the inside to accommodate more photos. Transfer a photo onto papyrus paper, then sew the paper to the cover of the mini book. Slip the journaling strip into a long glassine envelope. Add additional photos to the right side of the layout. Stephanie transferred one of the photos to give it a different look.*

3 MOM'S BOOK OF TREASURED WORDS
By Kris Stanger

Acrylic sealer: Decorative Crafts
Adhesive: Diamond Glaze, JudiKins;
Mod Podge, Plaid
Alphabet page pebbles, charmed photo
corners, defined sticker, eyelet letters,
eyelets, label holder, magnetic date
stamp, shaped clips, simply stated
rub-on and wire: Making Memories
Alphabet stamps: PSX Design
Antiquing gel and paint: Delta
Beads: Mill Hill
Computer font: Garamouche, P22
Conchos: Scrapworks
Fibers: On the Surface
Gold key: 7gypsies
Metal corners: Embellish It!,
Boutique Trims
Paper: Making Memories
Other: Chalk, jute and tissue paper

how to: Cut a front and back cover
from thin cardboard. Decoupage tissue
paper to the cardboard pieces. Add
filler pages. Mark holes for the binding,
punch with an anywhere punch and set
eyelets. Bind with jute. Score the cover
and the inside pages just to the right
of the binding. On the cover, hang
Eyelet Words from beaded wire and
place alphabet Page Pebbles behind
a label holder. Frame letters with
conchos, then fill with Diamond
Glaze. Add other embellishments
as desired.

4 MY SISTER, MY BROTHER, MY FRIEND
By Lynne Montgomery

Adhesives: Metal Glue, Making Memories;
Photo tape, 3L
Buttons: Dress It Up
Computer font: CK Italic, Creating
Keepsakes; Times New Roman
Defined stickers, eyelets, funky with
fiber, label holder and page pebble:
Making Memories
Dried foliage: Nature's Pressed
Jewelry tag: American Tag
Paper: Making Memories, 7gypsies,
Anna Griffin and Frances Meyer
Varnish: Right Step Varnish, J.W. etc.
Other: Charm, envelope, linen thread,
paint, transparency and twill tape

how to: Layer coordinating papers to
create a background. Tear and crumple
some of the edges to add texture.
Photocopy an entire Defined sticker
sheet onto a transparency. Adhere to an
envelope with spray adhesive and cut off
the excess. Adhere the envelope and
excess transparency, side by side, on
the layered background as if they were
continuous. Dry brush acrylic paint
around the edges. Cut out the envelope
flap opening in the transparency with an
X-Acto knife. Attach label holder and
title to twill tape using eyelets. Run the
twill tape around the entire layout, then
tuck a photo behind the tape. Attach
embellishments and use a photo-safe
varnish over the dried foliage.

Lynne's tip: For a refreshing change,
have someone else do the journaling.
In this case, Lynne had her children
write letters to each other telling what
they liked about the other person and
telling nice things the other person
has done for them.

3 journaling

Sometimes, journaling can feel like a homework assignment. It's not easy to do, but it's so important to include on layouts. It can be a few heartfelt words, random thoughts or a lengthy narrative. Whether sentimental or serious, reflective or funny, your thoughts and memories can be made more interesting, interactive and aesthetically pleasing through the use of attachments.

In the following pages, we've compiled creative and unusual ways of getting words down on the page. From a wire mesh corner pocket with a collection of torn word strips to loops of sherbet-colored beads for hanging tags and embellishments, you'll find plenty of ideas that make the grade. And don't worry—we won't check your grammar.

1 THE THRILL OF VICTORY
By Robin Johnson

Embossing enamel: Ultra Thick Embossing Enamel, Suze Weinberg
Eyelet shapes, jump rings, photo flips, ribbon, simply stated mini, staples, paper tag and wire mesh: Making Memories
Letter squares: Nostalgiques, EK Success
Mini-snowflake charm: Embellish It!, Boutique Trims
Paper: Making Memories
Stamping ink: Clearsnap

how to: *Adhere together 3" strips of white and green paper. Place the main photo on the pieces and tear down both sides. Randomly cut a piece of Wire Mesh that is the same length as the mat. Adhere mesh with staples or adhesive dots, then place the matted photo next to the mesh. Press snowflake Eyelet Shapes into white ink. Heat emboss, then tie to the Wire Mesh with ribbon or jump rings. Tie a tag to the mesh. For the journaling book, tear varying sizes of paper and fold in half. Attach a ski-lift ticket or other memorabilia to the cover. Set Photo Flips on the cover, then to the background page. Cut a strip of paper and rub on the Simply Stated phrase "the thrill of". Hang the title from a piece of Wire Mesh with jump rings.*

2 SNOW ADVENTURE
By Robin Johnson

Album: 7gypsies
Alphabet stamps: Postmodern Design and PSX Design
Brads, eyelets, label holder and snaps: Making Memories
Stamping ink: Ranger Industries
Other: Twine

how to: *Adhere a photo to the album cover. Tie twine around the front cover only. Mount a word strip behind a label holder. Attach with snaps. For the title, the same ink color was used to stamp "snow" and "adventure." To make the word "snow" lighter, stamp the word on scratch paper several times until you get the desired color. Stamp the word "adventure" on top. Add journaling, then attach with brads.*

3 CARMEL
By Robin Johnson

Canvas block: Canvas Concepts
Paint: Delta
Tag: Avery
Title sticker: Wordsworth
Twine: Hillcreek Designs
Washer word: Making Memories

how to: *Tape off the bottom edge of the canvas and paint. Paint the sides of the canvas and let dry. Cut photos to fit on canvas. Place a Wordsworth sticker over a photo. Adhere all photos to the canvas with adhesive dots. Cover a Washer Word with cream paint, then wipe off excess paint so it only stays in the grooves. Tie journaling tag to the washer. Hang washer from the top with twine. Paint a title at the bottom.*

4 NATURE'S GIFTS
By Robin Johnson

Metal finding: Karmul Studios
Paint: Delta
Snaps: Making Memories
Stamping ink: Clearsnap
Other: Foam board, shells and transparency

how to: *Cut foam board frame to size. Paint sides and top with blue paint and allow to dry. Age the edges with copper ink. Adhere to card. Adhere a photo inside the frame. Place seashells inside the frame. Print random words and phrases on a transparency. Cut to size, then place on top of the foam board. Using an X-Acto knife, cut small holes and push snaps in place to hold down the transparency. Adhere metal pieces at the top and bottom. Ink the edges of the card to age.*

2

1 UNOFFICIAL POSE
By Stephanie McAtee

Adhesive: Mod Podge, Plaid
Metal finding: Karmul Studios
Paint: Americana
Stick pin: Making Memories
Other: Burlap, chipboard and pieces
of an old metal frame

how to: *Cover chipboard with Mod
Podge. Lay burlap over the top, then
apply another layer of Mod Podge.
When dry, cover the burlap with acrylic
paint. To frame the focal photo, break
apart an old gold frame and flatten
with a hammer. Apply acrylic paint to
the surface, then rub some of it off so
the design in the frame stands out. For
the tag, walnut ink a large tag and fold
it in the shape of a matchbook. Staple
top fold down, and tuck larger fold
underneath. Punch a hole at the top
through both layers and wind the lace
through it. Tie a charm in the lace.
Journal and then hang with a straight
pin onto the page.*

2 BRIETTE—10 MONTHS OLD
By Rhonda Solomon

Beads, eyelet letter, label holder, magnetic
date stamp and simply stated rub-on:
Making Memories
Beads: The Beadery
Embossing powder: Posh Impressions
Paint: Delta
Stamping ink: Marvy
Other: Fabric

how to: *Paint an 11" square of fabric
white and let dry. Paint flowers and
leaves onto the fabric. Allow to dry, then
lightly dry brush with black paint. Print
journaling on cardstock and cut into tag
shapes. Edge with black ink. Machine
stitch photos onto the layout. Attach
journaling tags to the layout with beads.
Add tiny glass beads to the edges of
the layout. Heat emboss the Eyelet
Letter with peach-colored embossing
powder and attach to the layout with
beads. Paint the label holder with
acrylic paint. Let dry, then brush lightly
with black ink. Stitch into place with
thread and beads.*

3 SARAH
By Robin Johnson

Paint: Delta
Paper and vellum: Making Memories
Ribbon: Offray
Staples and paper tag: Making Memories
Sticker: Wordsworth
Other: Flowers and metal flower charm

how to: *Trim white paper and tear on two sides. Mount on green background. Place photo on page. Staple vellum strips over the photo. Paint name above the photo. Adhere flowers in place and staple a vellum strip over the stems. Tie a tag to the center flower. Put a quotation sticker on white paper and cut out. Mat with vellum and staple in the corners. Attach poem piece to page and add ribbons and flower charm to the top.*

4 QUOTATIONS
By Heidi Swapp

Brad, button, jump rings and shaped clips: Making Memories
Metal corners: Scrappy's
Ribbon: Offray
Other: Silk flower

how to: *Hand write or type inspirational quotations, then add interest with colored pencils. Mount each quotation on colored cardstock. Clip them together with Shaped Clips. Embellish with ribbons, silk flower and metal corner.*

1 A BOY'S WILL
By Lynne Montgomery

Computer font: CK Sketch, Creating Keepsakes; Times New Roman
Defined stickers, eyelets, jump rings and metal-rimmed tag: Making Memories
Hemp: Darice
Paper: Making Memories
Other: Book pages, paint, screen and scrim

how to: *Layer various papers and fabrics to create a background. Dry brush acrylic paint around the edges. Fold a piece of screen around the lower right corner, creating a pocket. Secure the screen to the back with tape, and machine stitch along the edges. To create the title, cut letters from magazines and attach to a vellum tag. Set eyelets in the vellum and secure tag to layout with hemp. Create a journaling block using the packing tape transfer method. (Using a photocopy of the journaling, place a piece of clear packing tape over the journaling block. Place the journaling block in water for a few minutes, then gently rub the paper backing off with your finger.) Secure the journaling block with eyelets and hemp. Cut words from a Defined sticker sheet and place in the pocket. Attach smaller Defined words to hemp with eyelets and jump rings.*

2 TAKE ME FISHING
By Kris Stanger

Adhesive: Diamond Glaze, JudiKins
Alphabet stamps: PSX Design
Computer font: 2Peas Flea Market, downloaded from www.twopeasinabucket.com
Glass beads: Halcraft
Mesh: Magenta
Metal words, page pebbles, shaped clips and snaps: Making Memories
Paint: Delta
Paper: Making Memories
Other: Fishing line

how to: *Use Diamond Glaze to adhere the glass beads to the paper. Paint the Metal Words with acrylic paint, then cover with Diamond Glaze to seal and add shine. Put page pebbles over each letter for the title and date. Tie shaped clips with fishing line.*

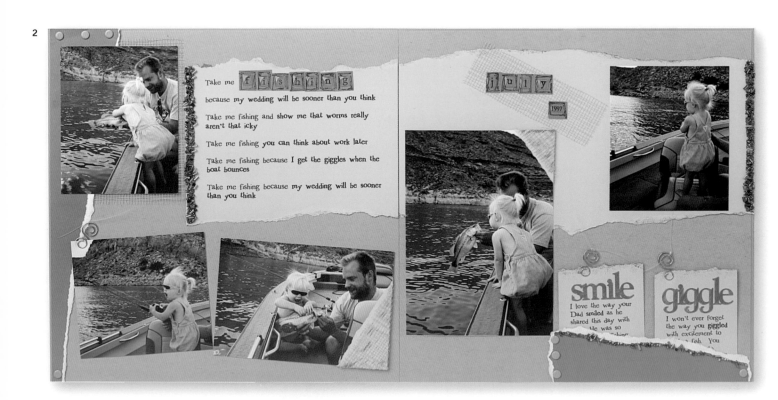

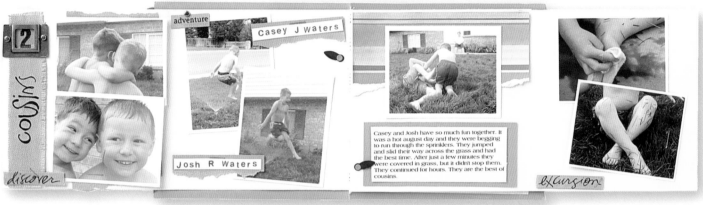

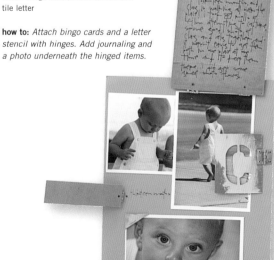

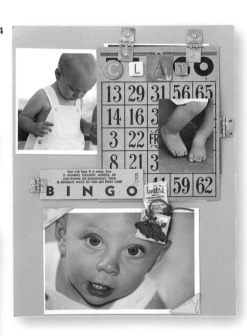

3 ADVENTURE BOOK

By Emily Waters

Alphabet stamps: Making Memories and Postmodern Design
Brads, defined sticker, eyelet charms, eyelet words, jump rings, label holders, magnetic date stamp, page pebble, photo anchors, ribbon, safety pins, simply stated rub-ons, snaps, staples and washer words: Making Memories
Paint: Delta
Paper: Making Memories and Bazzill Basics
Photo corners: Kolo
Other: Fabric and twine

how to: *Fold a piece of 6" x 12" card-stock in half. Create inside pages and machine stitch down the spine to bind. Attach a photo to the front using photo corners. Tear a Defined sticker and attach with a staple. Stamp the date on a circle Eyelet Charm, then add ribbon and safety pin. Fold the Eyelet Charm around the cover. Embellish the fold-out pages. Attach Photo Anchors just outside the fold-out pages so they can be held shut. Apply Simply Stated rub-ons to ribbon, then attach to the pages. Paint a strip of canvas fabric, then apply a rub-on. Stamp number, cover with a Page Pebble, then attach a label holder over the top using brads. Staple other photos and ribbon pieces as desired.*

4 CLAY

By Stephanie McAtee

Alphabet charms, hinges, snaps and staples: Making Memories
Metal finding: Karmul Studios
Leather pieces: Rusty Pickle
Paint: Americana
Paper: Making Memories and 7gypsies
Other: Bingo cards, letter stencil and tile letter

how to: *Attach bingo cards and a letter stencil with hinges. Add journaling and a photo underneath the hinged items.*

1 STUDIO
By Heidi Swapp

Alphabet stamps: Postmodern Design
Jump rings and ledger paper:
Making Memories
Paper: Chatterbox
Ribbon: Offray
Tags: American Tag
Other: Charms, fabric and metal plate

how to: *Attach journaling to the layout with jump rings, adding ribbon and charms to the jump rings. Rubber stamp the title with acrylic paint.*

2 SHE'S TWO
By Heidi Swapp

Alphabet stamps: Dawn Houser,
Inkadinkado
Bead chain, eyelet charm, eyelet letter,
eyelets, jump rings, metal-rimmed tag,
mini charmed plaque, simply stated
rub-ons, paper tag and washer word:
Making Memories
Paint: Plaid
Ribbon: May Arts
Tags: Avery
Other: Bingo card, definitions, envelope,
hooks and playing card

how to: *Triple mat an enlarged photo. Apply Simply Stated rub-ons to the photo. Adhere photo to background paper. Paint Bead Chain with three coats of acrylic paint. Let dry, then spray with a clear sealer. String Bead Chain across the layout. Hang various ephemera on the Bead Chain with jump rings, ribbon and hooks.*

3 HAPPY BIRTHDAY GIFT-CARD TAG
By Heidi Swapp

Beads: Beads by Pamela
Button, defined sticker, scrapbook
stitches and wire: Making Memories
Jewelry tag: American Tag
Paper: Bazzill Basics
Ribbon: Paper Source
Other: Charm and dye

how to: *Cut a tag from cardstock. Wrinkle and dye pink. Fold ribbon over the top and secure with a button and Scrapbook Stitches. Set four eyelets on the tag, then add wire in an X shape. Thread beads and a charm onto the wire. Slip a card behind the wire.*

4 WHEN I GROW UP
By Julie Turner

Acrylic gesso: Liquitex
Buttons, page pebble and simply stated
rub-on: Making Memories
Computer font: Arial Narrow
Paint: Golden Glaze, Golden Artist Colors
Paper: Making Memories
Ribbon: Bucilla
Typewriter keys: 7gypsies
Other: Canvas, linen thread and transparency

how to: *Use patterned paper to add two different textures to the layout. First, scan patterned paper, then print onto a transparency. Next, wet, crumple and iron the patterned paper to age. Layer the transparency and aged papers over canvas that has been painted with gesso. Add Page Pebbles to the tops of typewriter keys and apply Simply Stated rub-ons to the canvas. To make the colors on the page blend together, brush the buttons, cardstock and canvas with a light coat of Golden Glaze. Secure the journaling tag with a button.*

4 memorabilia

Brochures, maps, programs, ticket stubs, postcards-some might call it trash, but crafters call it treasure. And this chapter shows you how to get all that stuff out of boxes and into your scrapbook.

Photo Anchors™ and mismatched hardware get an A+ for holding stellar homework assignments in place. Interlocking Shaped Clips™ and knotted ribbon become an elegant, timeless tag top. And stitched see-through pockets housing various mementos create a visually pleasing border effect along the side of a page. With all the memorabilia you're accumulating, you have a golden opportunity for attachment creativity.

1 IN MEMORY
By Jennifer Jensen

Defined stickers, ribbon, shaped clip and staples: Making Memories
Paint: Delta
Paper: Making Memories
Other: Fabric, fabric tag, tulle and vellum

how to: *For the background, apply a thick layer of paint to cardstock. When partially dry, scrape most of it off. Sew tulle to the page corner to hold memorabilia. Create a photo mat from fabric and attach to layout with buttons and ribbon. Attach an embellished tag with a staple and create a tab for the obituary with a shaped clip and ribbon.*

2 BABY FEET
By Jennifer Jensen

Alphabet stamps: PSX Design
Iron-on transfer: Invent It
Metal sheets, page pebble and ribbon charms: Making Memories
Paint: Delta
Ribbon: Bucilla
Other: Canvas and glass

how to: *Transfer the baby feet onto canvas. Drill two holes in a piece of glass. Lace ribbon through two ribbon charms, then through the glass and iron-on transfer. Tie at the top. Make a small frame from Metal Sheets. Put a Page Pebble over the photo, then hang the frame from the ribbon. Stamp a name on metal and glue to the fabric.*

3 ONE YEAR TAG BOOK
By Jennifer Jensen

Charmed frame, defined sticker, eyelet charm, eyelet letters, eyelet word, funky with fiber, metal frames, metal words, magnetic date stamp, safety pins, staples and washer words: Making Memories
Paint: Delta
Silk ribbon: Bucilla
Other: Book ring, buttons, chenille, fabric, metal rings and pages from old children's book

how to: *Cut tags from various fabrics with pinking shears. Embellish the fabric with memorabilia for the child's first year of life. Sew the embellished fabric to green paper tags. Hold the tags together with a large book ring. Jennifer's tip: Print the photos in wallet size so they fit on the tags.*

4 GLIMPSE OF A YEAR
By Jennifer Jensen

Beads, eyelet, metal sheet, ribbon charms, safety pins and shaped clip: Making Memories
Paint: Delta
Ribbon: Bucilla
Other: Buttons, canvas, chenille, velvet ribbon and wooden block

how to: *Cut three separate pieces of chenille and canvas with pinking shears. Sew the three pieces of canvas together—with the chenille forming pockets—to create a pocket memorabilia book. Add memorabilia to the pockets and canvas. Create a closure by gluing two buttons together. Adhere to the right-hand flap. Tie ribbon around the buttons. Cut a wooden block in half, glue to the top of a button, then glue to the left flap. Wind ribbon around both sides to close.*

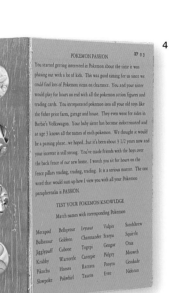

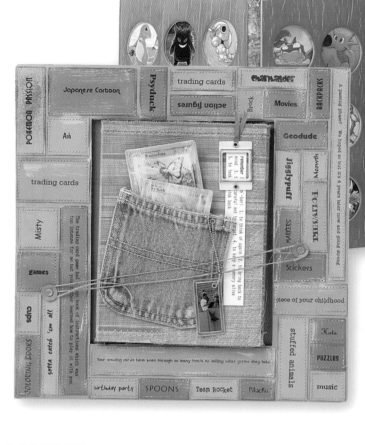

1 THE LION KING
By Rhonda Solomon

Charmed frame, eyelet tag alphabet, safety pin, shaped clips, snaps and staples: Making Memories
Embossing powder: Ranger Industries
Paint: Delta
Paper: Perspectives, Making Memories
Rubber stamps: Stampin' Up!
Thread: Hillcreek Designs
Other: Binding fabric

how to: Rubber stamp animal images and heat emboss with black powder. Accent each animal differently by trimming with pinking shears, adding netting or tearing. Place in Perspective openings. Add photos to layout. Attach binding tape with snaps and staples. Rubber stamp images on binding tape with acrylic paint. Mat memorabilia, then attach to layout with Shaped Clips. Emboss the edges of the layout with gold embossing powder.

2 COLTON'S FIRST DAY
By Heidi Swapp

Alphabet stamps: PSX Design
Metal-rimmed tags, photo anchors and snaps: Making Memories
Paper: Making Memories
Photo corners: Kolo
Walnut ink: Postmodern Design

how to: Age background papers with walnut ink. Age background strips with walnut ink. To create stripes, trim skinny pieces of varying colors of cardstock, age and attach to background strips. Adhere background strips to background paper. Secure memorabilia to the layout with Photo Anchors. Secure memorabilia to the layout with Photo Anchors.

3 FOCUS
By Stephanie McAtee

Adhesive: Diamond Glaze, JudiKins
Alphabet charms, jump rings and page pebbles: Making Memories
Football: Karmul Studios
Paint: Americana
Photo corners: 7gypsies
Other: Cardboard, lock and photo sleeves

how to: Fold cardboard to create a cathedral opening. Cut a rectangle in one of the flaps to expose a photo from the inside. Attach the bolt lock with screw posts. Hang the plastic schedule card with jump rings. Staple photo sleeves inside to house more photos and memorabilia.

4 POKEMON PASSION
By Lynne Montgomery

Adhesive: Duro Spray Adhesive, Manco; Perfect Paper Adhesive, USArtQuest
Bead chain, defined sticker, eyelets, label holder, metal-rimmed tag, snaps and staples: Making Memories
Computer fonts: Alba, Baby Druffy, Banjoman Open Bold, Bermuda Solid, Boulder, Calligrapher, Franciscan, GungshuChe, Heather, Jenkins v2.0, Jester, Lithographlight, Porky's, Pythagoras, Serifa BT, Space Toaster, Socket, Staccato 222BT, Teletype, Twentieth-Century Poster 1, Typo Upright BJ, Vagabond and Weltron Urban, downloaded from the Internet; Cezanne, P22; Comic Sans and Times New Roman; CK Constitution, CK Corral, CK Fresh, CK Fun, CK Lumpy, CK Sassy and CK Stenography, Creating Keepsakes
Embossing enamel: Ultra Thick Embossing Enamel, Suze Weinberg
Hemp: Darice
Paint: Americana
Paper: Making Memories
Stamping ink: Clearsnap and Ranger Industries
Other: Coin book, denim pocket, foam board, packing tape, Pokemon cards, ribbon and scrim

how to: To create the memorabilia holder, gently tear the cover off a coin book. Adhere patterned paper and scrim to the cover. Machine stitch to secure. Sew a denim pocket on the front and add embellishments. Paint the inside chipboard pieces with acrylic paint. When dry, rub a brown inkpad over the top and wipe off excess with a paper towel. Adhere pictures to the back of the chipboard so they show through the holes. Glue the chipboard pieces back inside the cover.

Trim cardstock 1/8" on all sides and cut a rectangular opening in the center so the coin book will fit inside. Type all words on the computer using various fonts. Cut one word into a rectangle, ink the edges, then attach to the background cardstock. Attach the words as you go so you can gauge what size the next rectangle should be. Machine stitch around each word block. Randomly and lightly apply acrylic paint over the words. Attach hemp on both sides of the opening with brads. Cut a piece of foam board slightly smaller than the cardstock. Cut an opening in the foam board slightly larger than the one in the cardstock. Glue the cardstock to the foam board. Adhere a coordinating cardstock to a piece of chipboard and place it behind the layout so it shows from the front.

Lynne's tip: Cut the cardstock and foam board down from its original size so the layout fits in a page protector.

1

where are you going?

PEBBLE BEACH

Pebble Beach Golf Course. Fabulous shops & views.

long trip up the coast to see

forget GOLF...
enjoy SHOP

August 2002

2

on the road to OXFORD

OXFORD

Paula Kremer
Mark & Shelly Sandstrand

laugh
FRIENDS
FUN

Andrew & Robin johnson

Ever had one of those times when you laughed so hard you cried? Our trip to Oxford was one long continuum of laughter and tears. From the amazing feat of packing the car (11 pieces of luggage and 5 adults in a Vauxhall), to going the wrong way down a one way street, to sharing "tourist" stories, to taking a wrong turn and not having an exit for 30 miles, it seemed like the journey that wouldn't end! Thank heavens we were with some dear friends who made the journey as fun as the destination.

OXFORD

september 2002

1 · PEBBLE BEACH
By Heidi Swapp

Alphabet stamps: PSX Design and
The Missing Link Stamp Company
Hinges, page pebbles and simply
stated mini: Making Memories
Paper: Making Memories
Ribbon: Paper Source
Other: Chipboard and map

how to: *Cover a piece of chipboard
with a map and secure to layout with
hinges. Add pictures underneath. Heidi
applied Page Pebbles over the cities
they visited.*

2 OXFORD
By Robin Johnson

Alphabet stamps: Postmodern Design
Hinges, label holder, metal frames, page
pebble, ribbon, snaps and paper tags:
Making Memories
Paint: Delta
Rubber stamps: Hero Arts, Inkadinkado
and Scrapbookin' Stamps
Stamping Ink: Ranger Industries
Other: Book-binding tape and string

how to: *To make the frames, sand Metal
Frames with a fine sandpaper. Paint the
frames and allow to dry. Stamp white
ink onto the painted frames and heat
set with white embossing powder. For
the postcard books, use book-binding
tape to attach the cards together at the
top. When the book is complete, attach
to the page with hinges so the postcards
open easily.*

3 MINNEAPOLIS
By Emily Waters

Alphabet stamps: PSX Design and
Postmodern Design
Artisan labels, Bead chain, brad,
charmed photo corners, ribbon, safety
pin, simply stated mini, snap and
staples: Making Memories
Paper: Making Memories and
Bazzill Basics
Walnut ink: Postmodern Design

how to: *Create a memorabilia flip chart
by cutting and sewing sheet protectors
together to create custom pockets.
Attach them all to a piece of cardstock,
then fold the top of the cardstock down
and staple. Stamp title on a piece of
fabric and dip in walnut ink to age.
Attach to cardstock with a safety pin.
Create a small accordion book by scoring
and folding a strip of paper that has
been cut to fit the photos. Attach the
back of the book to the page. Create a
closure with looped ribbon and a staple.
Loop the ribbon around a brad.*

4 FAVORITES AT FIVE
By Kris Stanger

Adhesive: Mod Podge, Plaid
Alphabet stamps: PSX Design
Eyelet letter, eyelets and shaped clip:
Making Memories
Mulberry paper: Provo Craft
Paper: Bazzill Basics
Rickrack: Wrights
Silk flowers: Darice
Stamping ink: Stampin' Up!
Other: Buttons, fabric, particle board
and ribbon

how to: *Cut a front and back cover
from particle board. Make the front
cover shorter than the back cover so
the sunflowers are visible when the
book is closed. Make the binding
piece from a strip of cardboard. Lay
the binding piece and front cover side
by side, leaving a narrow space in
between. Cover the two pieces with
mulberry paper and Mod Podge.
Create the inside pages from cardstock.
Stamp titles onto canvas, then sew
to the cardstock. Insert between the
covers, then drill holes for the binding.
Bind with ribbon. Cover the photo
with Mod Podge to add texture and to
protect the photo. Machine stitch the
sunflowers to a piece of muslin. Glue
the embellished muslin to the back
cover. Create tags from photos, artwork
and other memorabilia to slip in the
page pockets.*

3

4a

4b

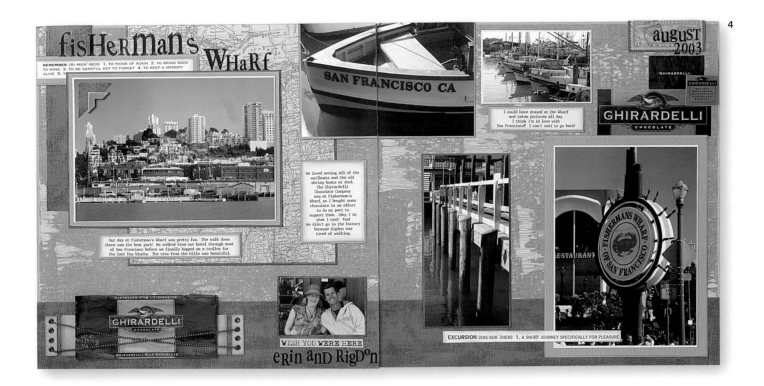

1 ADVENTURE: LOMBARD ST.
By Erin Terrell

Alphabet stamps: PSX Design
Defined stickers and washer words:
Making Memories
Mesh: Avant Card
Stamping ink: Clearsnap and Memories
Other: Fiber, handmade paper, tag and
walnut ink

how to: *Layer strips of blue and rust
colored cardstock and mesh. Mount
photo on cream, then rust-colored
cardstock. Mount again on textured
cardstock, then back it with more
rust colored cardstock. Punch holes
in paper and add Washer Words over
the holes. String fiber through the
washers to secure the photo. Ink the
edges of Defined stickers, then add to
page. Journal on a walnut-inked tag.
Add to fiber with a jump ring.*

**2 POSTCARDS FROM
SAN FRANCISCO**
By Erin Terrell

Alphabet stamps: PSX Design
Defined stickers, eyelet tag alphabet, eyelets,
photo flips, safety pin, snaps and washer
words: Making Memories
Mesh: Avant Card
Stamping ink: Memories; StazOn, Tsukineko
Other: Jute and postcards

how to: *Create an envelope from blue
papers and sand the edges. Embellish
with a postcard and Defined sticker. Tie
jute around the envelope and adhere a
Washer Word with a safety pin. Create
an accordion-fold album with paper and
Photo Flips. Trim postcards to fit the
pages and adhere with eyelets and jute.
Embellish the album with strips of
paper and mesh. Make the title by
stamping travel word definitions over
the "S" and "F" Eyelet Tag Alphabet
letters using StazOn ink. Adhere the
letters with snaps. Use alphabet stamps
for the rest of the title.*

3 ESCAPE ALBUM
By Erin Terrell

Album, charmed plaque, magnetic date
stamp, simply stated rub-ons and staples:
Making Memories
Fibers: Limited Edition Rubber Stamps
Ribbon: Offray
Stamping ink: Memories
Other: Handmade paper

how to: *Rub white ink over the front of
the album. Wrap a strip of decorative
handmade paper around the album
and secure with tape on the inside.
Rub white ink over the decorative
paper. Staple money to the front of
the album. Apply a Simply Stated
rub-on over the money and on the
album. Adhere a folded tag to the
decorative paper. Sand a Charmed
Plaque and frame it with cardstock.*

4 FISHERMAN'S WHARF
By Erin Terrell

Alphabet stickers: me and my BIG ideas
Bead chain, charmed photo corner, defined
stickers and eyelets: Making Memories
Computer font: Incognitype, downloaded
from the Internet
Paint: Plaid
Paper: me and my BIG ideas
Stamping ink: Clearsnap

how to: *Apply white paint to a blue
background. Layer strips of orange
cardstock to the blue paper. Add brown
ink to the orange strips. Adhere map
paper to background. Mat photos as
shown. Add a photo corner to focal
photo. Ink the edges of Defined stickers
and add to layout. Use eyelets and Bead
Chain to hold memorabilia in place.*

1

Spoiled Rotten by **GRAMMY**

enjoy   laughter   delight   happiness

Beach Memories

Love

TRAVEL
paradise

A mother becomes a true grandmother the day she stops noticing the terrible things her children do because she's so enchanted with the wonderful things her grandchildren do. — Lois Wyse

2

BASEBALL
sport
team TIGERS
coach 7 AUG 05
position ALL
mostly wins
record spring 2003

SOCCER
team Lightning
coach GREG
position ALL
win some
lose some
record Fall 2002

THE ROOKIE YEAR

3

5 books

Join the book club! Poetry or picture book, fiction or non-fiction, books make efficient use of space on a layout or stand alone as keepsakes of a special event. Have you ever thought of using an embellished magnetic clip to hold and display a volume of vacation photos? Or dangling a miniature recipe book with something so simple as a washer and Bead Chain™?

You'll see these and a wealth of other novel ideas in this chapter. Use them and your imagination when creating and attaching your next mini masterpiece.

1 SPOILED ROTTEN BY GRAMMY
By Heidi Swapp

Alphabet stamps: PSX Design
Artisan labels, charmed photo corners,
label holder, mini book, ribbon and
ribbon words: Making Memories
Photo corners: Kolo
Other: Charm

how to: *Attach the back cover of a mini book to the layout and fill with additional photos and journaling. Rubber stamp on Artisan Labels to create the page titles.*

2 PARADISE REFRIGERATOR MAGNET MINI BOOK
By Heidi Swapp

Alphabet stamps: Making Memories
Artisan label, defined stickers, eyelets,
jump rings, metal stamping die set,
mini charmed plaque, simply stated
rub-on and tag word: Making Memories
Paint: Plaid
Tag: Avery
Other: Beads, bulldog clip, ribbon
and twine

how to: *Remember a favorite trip or event with a mini book filled with photos and memorabilia. Embellish a magnetic clip with Defined stickers, ribbons and tags, then clip to the mini book. Stick the completed project to the fridge for easy access!*

3 THE ROOKIE YEAR
By Heidi Swapp

Alphabet stamps: Making Memories
and The Missing Link Stamp Company
Defined stickers and staples:
Making Memories
Photo corners: Kolo
Tag: Avery
Other: Book tape and envelopes

how to: *Alter a 6" x 8" envelope by cutting off the bottom and re-creating a new bottom flap. Create a tri-fold mini book to fit inside the envelope. Add additional photos to the mini book.*

1

1 CHERISH MEMORIES
By Emily Waters

Alphabet stamps: Postmodern Design and PSX Design
Artisan labels, brads, charmed frame, hinges, label holder, magnetic date stamp, metal-rimmed tags, page pebble, ribbon, simply stated rub-ons, staples and washer word: Making Memories
Paper: Making Memories
Other: Silk flower

how to: *Cut a hole in the striped paper for a photo. Trim around the outside edge of the striped paper. Wrap ribbon around the side and hang a vellum tag. Mount on solid paper. To create the mini book, cut a cover and inside pages as desired. Emily cut the inside pages from vellum and staggered the lengths to accommodate tabs. Fold small Artisan Labels around the vellum pages to create the page tabs. Sew all the inside pages together and attach to the cover using hinges. Add additional embellishments as desired.*

2 TEACH ME
By Jennifer Jensen

Artisan labels, defined stickers, label holder, metal stamping die set, page pebble, ribbon and scrapbook stitches: Making Memories
Chalk: Craf-T Products
Paint: Delta
Paper: Perspectives, Making Memories
Stamping inks: Daler-Rowney
Other: Grosgrain ribbon, lace and rhinestone flower

how to: *Place two photos behind two Perspectives openings. Mat a third photo with lace. Jennifer created a mini book with instructions on how to stitch (according to her daughter). Make the pages from canvas and back them with yellow fabric. The pages are bound together with ribbon.*

3 FRIENDS
By Jennifer Jensen

Eyelets, ribbon, ribbon charm, simply stated mini and staples: Making Memories
Paper: Making Memories
Other: Chenille, dictionary definition, flower and tulle

how to: *Sew a square of chenille on top of the front of a card. Set four eyelets on both sides of the fabric and string yellow ribbon through the card front as if tying a shoe. The ribbon will hold the mini book in place. Create a mini book from cardstock. Add a photo to the cover and frame with tulle. Embellish with a definition, ribbon and ribbon charm.*

4 PACIFIC OCEAN MEMORY COLLECTION
By Jennifer Jensen

Brads, defined stickers, hinges, jump rings, label holder, magnetic date stamp, metal sheet, metal stamping die set, mini charmed plaque, page pebble, photo anchor, simply stated mini and staples: Making Memories
Glass jar: Anchor Hocking
Paint: Delta
Paper: Making Memories
Other: Driftwood, fish net, piece of metal bucket, seashells, shell charm, tulle and twine

how to: *Arrange memorabilia and a photo in a jar. Braid twine and wrap it around the neck of the jar. Rub Simply Stated words directly onto the jar. To make the accompanying mini book, create a cover from a piece of scrap metal. Make the inside pages from cardstock and attach the pages together with hinges. Fashion a chain from jump rings and use it to hold the label holder to the cover.*

1

2

1 TAHITI
By Heidi Swapp

Colored pencils: Prismacolor
Elastics: 7gypsies
Eyelets and magnetic date stamp:
Making Memories
Jewelry tags: American Tag
Walnut ink: Postmodern Design
Other: Ribbon and string

how to: *Enhance tan paper by painting
it with walnut ink. Add elastics through
eyelets and use to hold memorabilia
to the page. Make a tab on the airline-
ticket envelope with folded paper and
an eyelet.*

2 YEAR 3
By Jennifer Jensen

#3 rub-on: Provo Craft
Embossing powder: Stampin' Up!
Hinges, jump rings, shaped clip, snaps
and staples: Making Memories
Paper: Making Memories
Other: Book paper and ribbon

how to: *To attach the title to the page,
make a chain with jump rings. Attach it
to a Shaped Clip placed at the top of
the title square. Attach the title square
to ribbon that has been wrapped around
the layout.*

3 HERSELF
By Stephanie McAtee

Adhesive: Diamond Glaze, JudiKins
Chain and corner finding: Karmul Studios
Paint: Americana
Paper: Making Memories
Small alphabet stamps: PSX Design
Stick pins and staples: Making Memories
Walnut ink: Anima Designs
Other: Buttons, large alphabet stamps,
pearls and ribbon

how to: *Attach a piece of chain to painted
chipboard with eye pins, allowing enough
space to hold a small matchbook-style
mini journal. Include thoughts, desires,
feelings, etc. about your station in
life. Add feminine embellishments to
complement the feel of the layout.*

4 BLACKBERRY HARVEST
By Kris Stanger

Acrylic matte sealer: Decorative Crafts
Adhesives: Diamond Glaze, JudiKins;
Mod Podge, Plaid
Alphabet charms, bead chain, charmed
frame, charmed photo corners, defined
stickers, simply stated rub-ons, shaped
clips, safety pin and washer word:
Making Memories
Alphabet stamps: PSX Design
Calendar: Nostalgiques, EK Success
Paint: Folk Art
Paper: Making Memories
Other: Beads and ribbon

how to: *Edge the background paper with
swashes of acrylic paint. Create a mini
book that contains favorite recipes.
Hang the book from Bead Chain and a
Washer Word. Add paint into the grooves
of the Alphabet Charms for interest.*

3a

3b

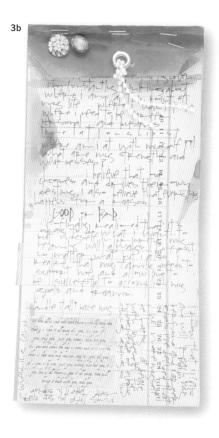

4a

4b

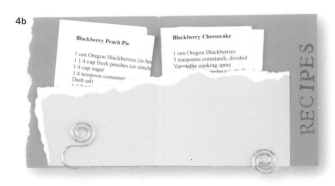

1a

1b

1 THE OLD STONE HOUSE
By Julie Turner

Computer fonts: Typewriter, P22;
Arial Narrow, WordPerfect
Eyelets, magnetic date stamp, safety
pin, simply stated rub-ons and wire:
Making Memories
Paint: Folk Art
Paper: Making Memories
Other: Keyhole charm, mat board,
microscope slides and twill tape

how to: *Lightly rub the cardstock with
medium-grade sandpaper to age. Add
depth to the layout by cutting a piece
of mat board to place underneath
the mat on the right side. To make
the microscope slides stand out from
the background, rub the edges with
a dab of acrylic paint. String wire
between two eyelets to make a hanger
for the mini book. The book can be
removed for reading.*

2 TEN REASONS YOU'RE
A GREAT SISTER
By Rhonda Solomon

Alphabet stamps: Hero Arts and
PSX Design
Beads: Magic Scraps
Button, eyelet, jump rings, metal word,
safety pin, shaped snaps, simply stated
rub-ons and staples: Making Memories
Paper: Karen Foster Design
Stamping ink: Marvy
Other: Card form, fabric and photo corners

how to: *Mat photo and place on card.
Print title on cardstock. Print one of
the title words on fabric and stitch to
cardstock. Rub a Simply Stated word
on fabric and stitch around the edge
to attach to the flap. To make the tag
book, attach rectangles of cardstock
together with jump rings. Print journaling
on cardstock and staple to the book's
pages. Attach the book to the card with
jump rings.*

2

3 CHERISH CARD WITH ALBUM
By Erin Terrell

Album: Maude Asbury
Defined sticker, eyelets, metal-rimmed tag, photo flips, shaped clip, simply stated rub-ons and snaps: Making Memories
Stamping ink: Tsukineko
Other: Corrugated paper and silk flower

how to: *Fashion a large card from purple cardstock. Apply white paint to the card. Add corrugated paper down the center of the card, then add white paint to that. Use Photo Flips to adhere an album to the front of the card. Adhere the Photo Flips to the album with adhesive dots so it can be removed from the card and used later. Add a metal-rimmed tag to the album with a Shaped Clip. Ink the edges of a Defined sticker and place on the tag. Attach a silk flower to the tag with a snap. Use a Simply Stated rub-on for the title.*

4 FINDING HER TALENT
By Robin Johnson

Alphabet charm, eyelets and ribbon: Making Memories
Alphabet stamps: PSX Design
Dried flowers: Pressed Petals
Metal corners: Magenta
Paint: Delta
Paper: Making Memories
Stamping ink: Ranger Industries
Tag: Avery
Other: Foam board and metal piece

how to: *To attach the small book, cut a piece of twill tape that is larger than the book. Using an anywhere hole punch, punch holes and set eyelets. Wind ribbon through the eyelets and through the ends of the metal piece. Tape ribbon to the back of the paper to secure. Add the Alphabet Charm letter to the center of the metal piece. Fill grooves of the letter with paint, then wipe off any excess. Off-set the main photo with colored paper and mount on foam board. Add metal corners. Cut squares of cardstock and glue pressed flowers to the center of the squares. Adhere squares to the page.*

1

Locks of Love

What a blessing it is for a mother to have a child understand the importance of sacrifice and giving. Crissy decided last summer to cut her hair short. Before she did it, she heard about "Locks of Love." It is a non-profit group that makes wigs for children in need. The hair you donate must be at least 10" long. So instead of getting it cut, Crissy let it grow out all summer to make sure it was long enough. The day finally came and she was a little nervous. But the joy on her face was real as they finished her cut. She knew she made a difference in someone's life. It was a wonderful gift and a privilege for me to be her mother.

delight

heaven sent
Love precious
the sweetest thing **Boy**

Lizzie's
Beauty Pageant
birthday party

make up, we did
painted nails.
we did it
all at Lizzie's
birthday
party. She was
just adorable
and then it
loved being
Beauty
Queen
for the
day.

APRIL 2003

3

sarah jane johnson

our little angel

4

6 accents

While journaling, titles and photos are the fundamentals of any layout, the accents are what bring it to life. And the method you choose to attach an object can be as clever and creative as the accent itself. Use Shaped Clips™ to hang vintage-inspired vellum tags or sandwich a flower-shaped eyelet in between a washer and eyelet to create a layered, three-dimensional look. You can even "cross-stitch" ribbon to anchor a frame, length of aged measuring tape or any other embellishment.

Whether your accents are sleek and sophisticated or cute and charming, attach them in a way that'll give your projects a personality all their own.

1 LOCKS OF LOVE
By Robin Johnson

Beads, eyelet letters, eyelets, metal word, ribbon and wire: Making Memories
Beads: Designs by Pamela
Embossing powder: Stampendous!
Heart: Provo Craft
Paint: Delta
Paper: Making Memories
Ribbon: Offray
Other: Flowers, jewel and waxed linen

how to: Tear a paper border strip. Braid hair and tie with elastics at each end. Punch holes through the paper and tie hair to paper with waxed linen. Cover with paper flowers. Cut strips of paper and use eyelets to attach them to the page. Thread beads onto wire, and string them across the strips. Adhere photos. Print journaling on a long strip of paper and attach with eyelets and ribbon. Cut off eyelet holes from some of the letters. Paint and heat emboss the letters and Metal Word. Attach to page with Metal Glue. Tie eyelet holes with ribbon and jewels. Tear corner pieces for photo and set eyelets on each side. Tie waxed linen through the eyelets. Tuck a metal heart behind the waxed linen.

2 BEAUTY PAGEANT PARTY
By Robin Johnson

Charms: Embellish It!, Boutique Trims
Jump rings, snaps and paper tag: Making Memories
Paint: Delta
Paper: 7gypsies
Other: Foam stamp, frame and ribbon

how to: Create a border with a foam stamp and paint. Paint a title and add a shadow with a black pen. Copy color photos in black onto colored cardstock. Outline the edges with a pen. Attach to the page with snaps to create the bottom border. Mat a small photo and adhere under title. Attach charms with jump rings through the holes in the ribbon. Add main photo and photo charm.

3 DELIGHT
By Robin Johnson

Photo anchors, scrapbook stitches, simply stated rub-ons and snaps: Making Memories
Stamping ink: Tsukineko
Other: Button, chenille, felt and frame

how to: Attach photo to background paper. Apply several Simply Stated phrases. Cut hearts from fabric. Attach chenille heart to paper and add Photo Anchors. Hand stitch around the felt heart, add an antique button and glue to paper. Place in frame. Rub the edges of the frame with stamping ink to age and add color.

4 OUR LITTLE ANGEL
By Robin Johnson

Alphabet stamps: PSX Design
Metal corners: Karmul Studios
Paint: Delta
Ribbon: Offray
Snaps: Making Memories
Stamping ink: Tsukineko
Other: Frame, heart, lace, paper flowers and waxed linen

how to: Paint a papier-mâché frame. When dry, sand off some of the color. Attach metal corners with Metal Glue. Add photo. Arrange flowers on the side and secure with lace and snaps. (The snaps will push through the papier-mâché.) Hang the heart from a snap with waxed linen. Add a ribbon tie. Stamp words around the frame opening.

3 FROM THE MOUTH OF BABES
By Lynne Montgomery

Adhesive: Metal Glue, Making Memories
Alphabet stamps: PSX Design
Computer font: CK Italic, Creating Keepsakes
Eyelets, page pebble, ribbon charm, staples and washer words: Making Memories
Paint: Americana and Jacquard Products
Paper: Making Memories and Anna Griffin
Pens: EK Success
Stamping inks: Ranger Industries
Tin ceiling: House Works
Other: Book paper, doily, flowers, packing tape, ribbon, scrim, tape measure and transparency

how to: *Cut patterned papers into various sizes of squares and rectangles. Piece the papers together, sewing the wrong sides together. If using lightweight papers, adhere to a heavier piece of cardstock before sewing. Cut a tin ceiling piece into a square and paint with acrylic paint. When dry, cut in half diagonally to form two triangles. Layer paper, material, transparency, corners and tape measure. Machine stitch to the background papers. Journal on tags and attach to layout with Washer Words and eyelets.*

Lynne's tip: The title was originally much larger, so she shrunk it on a copy machine, then used the packing tape transfer method to transfer it to the tag.

4 BEAUTY
By Lynne Montgomery

Adhesive: Decoupage & Collage Gel, Hot Off The Press
Alphabet stamps: PSX Design
Clear acrylic sealer: Plaid
Eyelets and label holder: Making Memories
Paper: Making Memories
Stamping ink: Ranger Industries
Other: Bottle, newspaper and ribbon

how to: *Decoupage newspaper strips onto a bottle. When dry, spray with an acrylic sealer. Stamp a title on patterned paper. Attach title to the back of the label holder with eyelets. Wrap ribbon around the bottle and through the eyelets. Tie the ends off with a knot.*

5 MINI ENCAPSULATED COLLAGES
By Lynne Montgomery

Adhesives: Decoupage & Collage Gel, Hot Off The Press; Duro Spray Adhesive, Manco Inc.; Foam Squares, Making Memories
Angel wings: Midwest Design
Beads, brad, button, charmed frame, eyelet letter, eyelet quote, ribbon charms, simply stated mini, tag and washer words: Making Memories
Clear acrylic sealer: Plaid
Computer font: Teletype
Dried foliage: Nature's Pressed
Embossing enamel: Ultra Thick Embossing Enamel, Suze Weinberg
Matte medium: Golden Artist Colors
High-gloss finish: EnviroTex
Marble: Panacea Products
Paint: DecoArt and Jacquard Products
Paper: Making Memories, 7gypsies and Anna Griffin
Ribbon: May Arts and Offray
Stamping ink: Clearsnap, Postmodern Design and Ranger Industries
Other: Bottle cap, charms, fiber, flowers, metal corner, newspaper, postage stamp, postcards, scrim, tins and tinker pin

how to: *Decoupage, paint or heat emboss a small metal tin. Line the inside of each tin with patterned paper that has been treated with a matte medium. (The paper won't show up as well if it is not treated, and if you're using a picture from a magazine, the flip side will show through unless treated first.) Assemble a mini collage in the tin, making sure everything is well adhered or it will float to the top. Following the manufacturer's directions, pour EnviroTex high-gloss finish over the collage, then let it cure.*

Lynne's tip: Before using the high-gloss finish, read the manufacturer's instructions very carefully. Mixing properly is very important. Lynne found that the better she mixed, the less bubbles she encountered later. She also found it easier to mix smaller portions. Experiment on one first so you can get a feel for how the chemicals react.

1 FAVORITES AT 5
By Emily Waters

Alphabet stamps: PSX Design
Brad, button, eyelet charm, label holder, ledger paper, magnetic date stamp, metal-rimmed tags, oversized page pebble, ribbon, safety pins, snap, staples and washer word: Making Memories
Paper: Making Memories
Other: Chipboard, fabric, silk flower and tag

how to: *Cut a large hole from a piece of chipboard to accommodate your photo. Rub chipboard with paint and rough up the edges for a worn look. Print text onto old ledger paper and attach down the side of page using various embellishments.*

2 T42
By Lynne Montgomery

Adhesive: Decoupage & Collage Gel, Hot Off The Press
Alphabet charms and charmed frames: Making Memories
Charms: Embellish It!, Boutique Trims
Flower: Offray
Paper: Making Memories
Ribbon: May Arts
Other: Box, chicken wire, clips, dried lavender, frame, newspaper, paint, tea bags, teacup hooks, tea spoon and wire

how to: *Staple chicken wire to the back of an old frame. Roll newspaper and fold down the top, forming a holder for dried flowers. Tie to chicken wire with ribbon. Decoupage one of the frames with paper from tea bag packaging. When dry, lightly dry brush with acrylic paint. Insert photos into frames and clip to chicken wire. Adhere Alphabet Charm title to frame with adhesive dots. Cover a small wooden box with patterned paper. Screw teacup hooks on the bottom to hang charms. Using wire, tie the box to the chicken wire. With a glue gun, adhere various tea bags and tea bag packages to the inside of the box. Glue a teaspoon to the side of the box and tie with ribbon.*

1 LITTLE GIRL REMEMBER THIS
By Erin Terrell

Brads, charmed photo corners, eyelets, jump rings, label holder, metal-rimmed tags, ribbon, ribbon words, safety pins, shaped clips and simply stated rub-ons: Making Memories
Charms and mesh: JewelCraft
Computer font: Incognitype, downloaded from the Internet
Paint: Americana
Paper: Michelle Anderson, Provo Craft
Stamping ink: Clearsnap
Other: Vintage handkerchief

how to: *Create a background from mesh and patterned papers. Mat photos as shown. Ink the edges of the journaling blocks and use Simply Stated rub-ons to create the title. Add Simply Stated rub-ons to vellum tags. Set an eyelet in each tag. Tie ribbon through the eyelets, hang the tags from Shaped Clips, then attach to the page with a brad. Attach a charm to the ribbon with a safety pin and jump ring. Frame a Ribbon Word with a label holder. Add a handkerchief to the upper corner and secure with tape on the back. Paint two Charmed Photo Corners with white paint, then add to one of the photos.*

2 BE GOOD TO YOUR MOM
By Heidi Swapp

Alphabet stamps: Piccadilly
Buttons, hinges, jump ring, label holder, ledger paper, photo anchors, safety pins, snaps, staples and washer words: Making Memories
Paint: Delta
Ribbon: May Arts
Tag: Avery
Other: Fabric and fusible web

how to: *Using fusible web, iron fabric to cardstock, overlapping pieces. Affix overlapping sections of fabric to the paper with mini buttons. Cover an extra piece of cardstock with fabric in the same way to make a flap that opens. Use another piece of fabric as a photo mat, and pin ribbon into place as photo corners.*

3 EIGHT REASONS YOU'RE GREAT
By Rhonda Solomon

Alphabet stamps: PSX Design
Brads, eyelet shapes, ribbon, ribbon
charms, safety pins, scrapbook stitches,
staples, washer word and wire word:
Making Memories
Burlap: Magic Scraps
Buttons: Hillcreek Designs
Embossing enamel: Ultra Thick Embossing
Enamel, Suze Weinberg
Paper: Anna Griffin, Bazzill Basics and
K & Company
Stamping ink: Tsukineko
Transparencies: Hammermill
Other: Jewelry tags and seam binding

how to: Create a photo mat from
cardstock. Hand stitch the inside
edge with Scrapbook Stitches.
Machine stitch seam binding to
the outside edge. Trace a large
flower shape on cardstock and
cut out. Ink the edges and heat
emboss. Hand stitch the inside of
the flower with Scrapbook Stitches.
Place printed papers on background
and add a burlap strip. Print title
and journaling on a transparency.
Attach to layout with ribbon, staples
or buttons. Rubber stamp name
on jewelry tags and attach to
frame with safety pins.

4 FRESH TAG
By Sharon Lewis

Charmed frame, defined sticker and
ribbon: Making Memories
Foliage stickers: Real Flower Stickers
Paint: Delta
Paper: Making Memories
Stamping ink: Clearsnap
Other: Buttons and newsprint paper

how to: Cut a tag shape from pink
paper. Cut another tag shape from
tan cardstock slightly larger than the
pink tag. Tear a corner piece from a
coordinating color of cardstock. Drag
an inkpad around all the edges, then
adhere the tag together. Machine
stitch around the perimeter. Paint
the Charmed Frame design with acrylic
paint, wiping excess paint from the
surface with a wet wipe. Cut newsprint
paper to fit the frame and attach a
flower sticker. Position frame on the
tag, slide ribbon through the frame
sides and around the tag. Adhere
newsprint accent to the frame with
adhesive dots, then adhere the frame
to the tag. Stitch buttons and ribbons
at the sides of the frame and at the top
of the tag to form the loop. Embellish
with a leaf sticker and a Defined sticker.

4

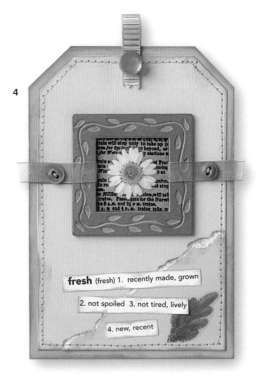

1 SOPHIE FRAME
By Sharon Lewis

Adhesive: Metal Glue, Making Memories;
Mod Podge, Plaid
Chalk and metallic rub-ons: Craf-T Products
Clasp: ScrapWorks
Defined stickers, eyelet phrase, eyelet tag
alphabet, eyelet word, hinges and ribbon:
Making Memories
Flash card: Manto Fev
Paint: Plaid
Photo corners: Boston International Inc.
Postage art: FoofaLa
Other: Wooden frame

how to: *Sand a wooden frame, then paint with two coats of dark brown paint. Let dry, then paint with two coats of light blue paint. When dry, sand the frame to expose some of the brown paint and natural wood. Attach postage art to the corner with Mod Podge, wrapping the excess picture around the edge. Chalk the Defined stickers, then attach to the frame. Paint the entire surface of the frame with Mod Podge. Tie ribbons to the Eyelet Tag Alphabet letters and attach the tags to the frame with pop-up adhesive dots. Attach hinges to the flash card with Metal Glue. Cut a navy blue mat slightly larger than the flash card and glue the hinges to the mat. Attach a photo behind the flash card. Brush acrylic paint over the Eyelet Phrase and Eyelet Word. When dry, set on the background cardstock, then attach the flash card and mat to the background cardstock. Frame and enjoy!*

2 SOFT & SWEET
By Jennifer Jensen

Artisan label, brads, funky with fibers, metal mesh, safety pin, staples, straight pin, woven label: Making Memories
Walnut ink: Postmodern Design
Other: denim, washer

how to: *Cut tag out of cardstock. Put a strip of metal mesh across the bottom. Stitch denim on tag turning up bottom edge. Staple down the side. Walnut ink your artisan labels. Attach artisan label with a brad on the side of the tag and tuck a photo in the pocket. Use a brad and a straight pin to hold woven label in place. Wrap artisan label across the top and secure with a brad. Use artisan label for a title on the bottom and hold in place with safety pin, fiber and a washer.*

3 BELIEVE
By Stephanie McAtee

Adhesive: Diamond Glaze, JudiKins
Eyelet shape, eyelet word, eyelets, page
pebble, simply stated mini and staples:
Making Memories
Paper: Making Memories
Printed twill and waxed linen: 7gypsies
Slide holder and walnut ink: Anima Designs
Tag: Avery
Other: Mirror-hanging hardware

how to: *Decoupage a double slide
holder with baseball ephemera.
Attach printed twill to the top.
Secure the slide holder to the
layout with mirror-hanging
hardware and waxed linen.*

4 BABY BROTHER
By Kris Stanger

Computer font: 2Peas Tiny Tadpole, down-
loaded from www.twopeasinabucket.com
Craft enamel: Krylon
Eyelet letters, oversized page pebble,
photo anchors, simply stated rub-ons,
snaps, stick pins, sticker letters and
paper tags: Making Memories
Fiber: On the Surface
Paint: DecoArt
Paper: Making Memories
Stamping ink: Stampin' Up!
Other: Buttons, muslin, postage stamp,
velveteen paper and vintage postcard

how to: *Cut a large square from the
middle of dark blue cardstock. Adhere
to tan paper and straight stitch around
the border. Attach Photo Anchors to the
side with fiber. Apply Simply Stated
rub-ons to the photos. Add photos and
other embellishments to the layout.*

*Kris' tip: When machine stitching
smaller pieces to a layout, such as
the "baby" square on this layout, sew
on a big piece, then trim it down so
the paper is easier to maneuver through
your machine.*

4

7 pockets/miscellaneous

Pockets are the ultimate accessory-they're as functional as they are fashionable. Holding everything from coins to cosmetics, pockets adorn pants, shirts, purses, and yes, even scrapbook pages.

Make a fashion statement on your projects using a "pocket-within-a-pocket" technique to contain elements on your page or design an album cover with a clear compartment made from the tiniest of eyelets. This chapter also details how to attach a row of fabric pockets to a distressed message board that's both practical and pretty. Try out (or try on) any of the following ideas and you'll create keepsakes that will never go out of style.

1 SAN FRANCISCO FAVORITES
By Heidi Swapp

Alphabet stamps: Postmodern Design
Artisan labels, brads, jump rings,
label holder, ribbon and shaped clip:
Making Memories
Fabric paper: K & Company
Paint: Delta
Stamping ink: Anna Griffin
Studs: Dritz
Tag: Avery

how to: *Lightly dye cream-colored cardstock with pink dye. Iron to dry. Mount dyed paper and fabric paper on cardstock to create a background. Attach photos by crossing ribbon over the top and securing with studs. Rubber stamp the word "favorite" with acrylic paint and ink the edges of the layout with a maroon ink pad.*

2 WALL-HANGING PHOTO BOOK
By Heidi Swapp

Fabric paper: K & Company
Brads, eyelet word, label holder,
simply stated mini and washer words:
Making Memories
Ribbon: Oh Boy!

how to: *Machine stitch up the center of several 6" x 12" pieces of cardstock to create a 6" x 6" mini book. Insert favorite photos and memories. Attach a ribbon hanger with brads and Washer Words.*

3 COLLIN
By Heidi Swapp

Brads, photo anchors and snaps:
Making Memories
Elastic: Britex Fabrics
Paper: Making Memories
Other: Dictionary paper

how to: *Adhere the elastic with ultra-sticky tape and snaps. Cut out words from the dictionary and adhere them to the Photo Anchors. Attach the Photo Anchors with mini brads.*

1 DISCOVER THE FUTURE
—REMEMBER WHEN
By Stephanie McAtee

Alphabet stamps: PSX Design
Bottle cap: Manto Fev
Defined sticker, jump rings, photo anchors,
snaps and washer word: Making Memories
Paint: Americana
Rubber band, silver bars and tissue paper:
7gypsies
Walnut ink: Anima Designs
Other: Cardboard, envelopes, newspaper
pieces and polymer clay

how to: *Stephanie created this portfolio
to showcase some of her son's senior
pictures. To make a similar portfolio,
cut cardboard to create a piece that
you have to open different areas to
get the whole visual effect. When it
is closed, it measures 12" x 12".
Journal on the portfolio and tuck
notes into the envelopes.*

2 THE NATURAL MAN
By Lynne Montgomery

Alphabet stamps: PSX Design
Buttons: Dress It Up
Computer font: Teletype
Eyelet, jump rings, magnetic date stamp,
metal mesh, metal-rimmed tag and safety
pin: Making Memories
Hemp: Darice
Label: me and my BIG ideas
Paper: Making Memories
Stamping ink: Postmodern Design and
Ranger Industries
Other: Burlap

how to: *Rumple the edges of the
background paper and age with ink.
Fold a strip of burlap around one side
of a piece of Metal Mesh. Hand stitch
burlap into place, adding buttons as
you go. Layer photo mat, photo and
Metal Mesh on background paper, then
tack in place. Cut a corner from burlap
and machine stitch in place. Stitch two
buttons on the left side and loop hemp
around each button to form a figure
eight. Attach tags to the hemp. Print
journaling onto walnut-inked paper,
then cut into strips. Zigzag stitch one
end of each strip to the layout. Insert
the other end into the burlap.*

3 CHINATOWN
By Erin Terrell

Computer font: Incognitype, downloaded from the Internet
Embossing powder: Ranger Industries
Eyelet charms, eyelet tag alphabet, eyelets and snaps: Making Memories
Oriental ephemera: Dibona Design
Paint: Americana
Paper: Making Memories and Paper Reflections
Ribbon: Offray
Rubber stamps: Hero Arts and Stampa Rosa
Stamping ink: Memories and Tsukineko

how to: *Dry brush red cardstock to create the background. Layer other papers and ephemera as shown. Rubber stamp text onto Eyelet Tag Alphabet letters using StazOn ink. Add to layout with snaps. Create pockets on the layout with ribbon or strips of paper and eyelets. Slip photos and memorabilia into the pockets. Paint the flower Eyelet Charms and allow to dry. Rubber stamp text onto the painted flowers with StazOn ink. Dip the flowers in a VersaMark ink pad, pour clear embossing powder over the top, then heat emboss. Attach the flowers with snaps.*

4 JULIETTE & GG'S HATS
By Sharon Lewis

Adhesive: Mod Podge, Plaid
Eyelets, label holder, ribbon words and rings: Making Memories
Old book page: Manto Fev
Page protector: C-Line
Paper: Making Memories
Other: Book paper and chipboard

how to: *Cut a front and back cover from chipboard, then cover with patterned paper. Trim photo to size, then cut a page protector 1/3" larger on each side to create a pocket. Position the photo between the front and back of the page protector. Mat the pocket on book paper and cardstock. Adhere the mats together, then cover with Mod Podge. Set mini eyelets around the sides and bottom of the pocket, attaching it to the mat. Adhere the pocket accent to the cover with Mod Podge. Paint the entire front cover with Mod Podge. Attach a Ribbon Word border with adhesive dots and attach the label holder with eyelets. Punch holes near the left edge and bind with rings.*

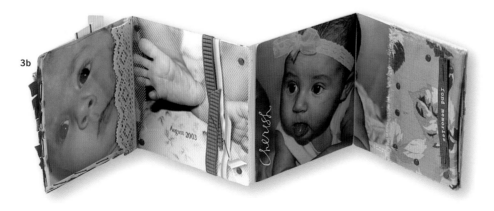

1 **SIMPLE MEMORIES**
By Emily Waters

Alphabet stamps: Making Memories
Artisan labels, brads, photo anchors,
ribbon words, safety pins, shaped clip,
simply stated rub-ons, staple and
stick pin: Making Memories
Other: Burlap

how to: *To create the pocket, sew a strip
of burlap onto chipboard. (Sew down
both sides and across the bottom.)
Then sew down both sides of the
center to create the pockets, folding
down a portion of the top for added
dimension. Add a t-pin, safety pin
and Shaped Clip to the pockets. Tuck
small photos in each pocket. Attach
remaining photos using Photo Anchors
or Ribbon Words and brads. Apply a
Simply Stated rub-on for the title. For
a finishing touch, add small amounts
of paint to the edges of the page.*

2 **RYLIE BOOK BOX**
By Jennifer Jensen

Brad, charmed frame, eyelet letters,
funky with fiber, hinges, jump rings,
ribbon, safety pin, snaps and staples:
Making Memories
Paint: Delta
Other: Box, charm, fabric, silk flower
and tulle

how to: *Paint a box with acrylic paint.
(Jennifer painted an empty rubber
stamp box). When dry, cut off one side
from the lid, then glue hinges to the
top of the box and to the bottom to
connect the two pieces. Set snaps in
each corner of the lid. Glue down a
painted Charmed Frame, adding jump
rings underneath each corner. Attach
the frame to the snaps with fiber.
Cut the top off the plastic square of
a Stitched Tin Tile package. Glue to
the frame to create a pocket. Fill the
pocket with tags and a charm.*

3 **RYLIE BOOK**
By Jennifer Jensen

Adhesive: Mod Podge, Plaid
Artisan label, defined sticker, magnetic
date stamp, metal frame, ribbon, simply
stated mini, snaps, staples and paper tag:
Making Memories
Paint: Delta
Paper: Making Memories
Other: Fabric, lace, tulle and vinyl

how to: *Create an accordion-fold book
to fit inside the box. Glue the back page
to the bottom of the box. For the front
pocket, cut off one side of a Metal
Frame. Decoupage fabric to the metal.
Glue pieces of ribbon to the back of
the frame. Slide a piece of vinyl under
the inside edges of the frame. Attach
the vinyl with staples to create a pocket.
Add photos and journaling throughout
the book and embellish as desired.*

4 POCKETS BULLETIN BOARD
By Jennifer Jensen

Adhesive: Mod Podge, Plaid
Bead chain, defined stickers, eyelet charms, eyelets, label holders, metal frames, metal-rimmed tags, metal sheets, page pebbles, ribbon, ribbon charms, simply stated mini, snaps, staples, stick pins and paper tag: Making Memories
Paint: Delta
Ribbon: Making Memories
Sealer and spray paint: Krylon
Other: Buttons, cork board, dictionary definitions, fabric, lace, tulle and window frame

how to: *Remove the glass from an old window frame. Cover cork board with fabric and attach to the back of the window. To make the pockets, cover Metal Frames with fabric. Add eyelets on both sides to attach the pockets to one another and connect them with spray painted Bead Chain. For the first pocket, decoupage three strips of ribbon, then sew on the "Notes" strip of paper. Add a Page Pebble and attach a label holder with ribbon. To make the second pocket, paint a heavy coat of Mod Podge over a Defined sticker. Let dry, then peel off most of the backing. You may need to slightly wet it to get the paper off. Decoupage it back onto the fabric pocket. Cut a hole in the center of a Metal Sheet. Fold out the sides, rub with acrylic paint and glue in place. For the fourth pocket, paint a tag Eyelet Charm with acrylic paint. Fold a dictionary definition and glue to tag. Add ribbon and Ribbon Charm. To make the fifth pocket, glue magazine letters to a square tag. Attach a label holder over the top with ribbon. For the push pins, glue painted flower Eyelet Charms to clear push pins and glue beads to the tops of Stick Pins.*

5 MY THOUGHTS
By Jennifer Jensen

Adhesive: Mod Podge, Plaid
Artisan label, defined stickers, eyelet charms, magnetic date stamp, metal-rimmed tag, metal stamping die set, simply stated rub-ons and staples: Making Memories
Paint: Delta
Paper: Making Memories
Wood ornament: Ornamental Mouldings
Other: Buttons, contact paper, fabric, flower, stencil and vinyl pocket

how to: *Cover a strip of cardstock with Defined stickers, then sand with sandpaper and cover with contact paper. Decoupage a square of fabric to the top of the background paper. Let dry, then staple the cardstock strip to the bottom of the page to form a pocket.*

5

Jenn Jensen

have fun
preserving memories forever
heidi swapp

in·spire' (in·spir'),
influence as if by a hi
dream (drēm), n
tures, or feelings
sleep. 2. Hence,

en·joy' (en·joi'), v.
to enjoy the picnic.
satisfaction; as, he

emily waters

the things I love right now:
san francisco
butterflies
wildflowers
snowflakes
long eyelashes
savannah, ga
windmills
"law and order"
leopard print
stained glass
lots of sleep
and my family

ERIN

Love

family
RHONDA
camera
Solomon
Sunday
sisters
kay
GAP
scrapping

julie turner
scrapbooking
since 1964

born & raised
in eureka ca
missionary
byu graduate
2nd grade teacher
wife & mother of 3
scrapbook enthusiast
8 year arizonan

lynne

my journey

GO CONFIDENTLY
IN THE
DIRECTION
OF
YOUR DREAMS
LIVE THE LIFE
IMAGINED

STEPH

Sharon

914 Summer Field

enjoy

each
moment

Suomi Finland 83 1,30

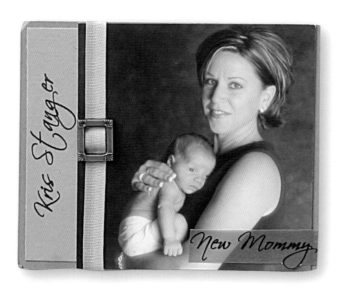

Kris Stanger

New Mommy

Erin Trimble   Jennifer Kofford

writers